First World War
and Army of Occupation
War Diary
France, Belgium and Germany

38 DIVISION
Divisional Troops
Divisional Trench Mortar Batteries
5 April 1916 - 31 January 1919

WO95/2546/4

The Naval & Military Press Ltd
www.nmarchive.com
Published in association with The National Archives

Published by

The Naval & Military Press Ltd

Unit 10 Ridgewood Industrial Park,

Uckfield, East Sussex,

TN22 5QE England

Tel: +44 (0) 1825 749494

www.naval-military-press.com

www.nmarchive.com

This diary has been reprinted in facsimile from the original. Any imperfections are inevitably reproduced and the quality may fall short of modern type and cartographic standards.

© Crown Copyright
Images reproduced by permission of The National Archives, London, England, 2015.

Contents

Document type	Place/Title	Date From	Date To
Heading	WO95/2546/4		
Heading	38th Division Divl Artillery 38th Trench Mortar Bty 1916 Apl-1919 Jan		
Heading	T M B 38 Div Art July 1917		
War Diary	Gore	05/04/1916	17/04/1916
War Diary	Laventie	01/05/1916	30/05/1916
Heading	38th Divisional T M Batteries. June 1917 Vol 12		
War Diary	Steentje Farm Camp Sheet 28 A 17 d.9.2	01/06/1917	30/06/1917
War Diary	A 17.a.9.1 Sheet 28	01/07/1917	14/07/1917
War Diary	C 19.a.0.3 Sheet 28. NW.	15/07/1917	16/07/1917
War Diary	C 19.a.0.3	16/07/1917	25/07/1917
War Diary	C 19.a.0.3 Sheet NW	26/07/1917	30/07/1917
War Diary	A 17.a.9.1	31/07/1917	31/07/1917
Heading	38 Divisional T.M. Instructions July 1917 I		
Miscellaneous	38th Divisional Trench Mortar Batteries. Instructions No. 1		
Miscellaneous	38th Divisional Trench Mortar Batteries. Ammunition Supply.	10/07/1917	10/07/1917
Miscellaneous	38th Divisional Trench Mortar Batteries. Addenda To T.M. Instructions No 1	10/07/1917	10/07/1917
Miscellaneous	Ammunition Supply	08/07/1917	08/07/1917
Miscellaneous	38th Divisional Trench Mortar Batteries. Instructions No. 2	13/07/1917	13/07/1917
Miscellaneous	Instruction. No. 2. Appendix "A"		
Heading	Bombardment Programme July 1917. II		
Miscellaneous	38th Divisional Trench Mortar Batteries.	06/07/1916	06/07/1916
Miscellaneous	A Form. Messages And Signals		
Miscellaneous		13/07/1917	13/07/1917
Operation(al) Order(s)	Right Artillery Trench Mortar Batteries. Operation Order No. 2	16/07/1917	16/07/1917
Miscellaneous	Right Artillery Trench Mortar Batteries.	19/07/1917	19/07/1917
Miscellaneous	Right Artillery Trench Mortars.	18/07/1917	18/07/1917
Miscellaneous	Right Divisional Artillery Trench Mortars.	17/07/1917	17/07/1917
Miscellaneous	Scheme For The Bombardment	16/07/1917	16/07/1917
Miscellaneous		15/07/1917	15/07/1917
Operation(al) Order(s)	38th Divisional Trench Mortar Batteries. Operation Order No. 1	14/07/1917	14/07/1917
Miscellaneous	Bombardment Scheme. Heavy T. M. Group. Right Division.	13/07/1917	13/07/1917
Miscellaneous	Right Artillery Trench Mortars	21/07/1917	21/07/1917
Miscellaneous	Right Artillery Trench Mortar Batteries.	22/07/1917	22/07/1917
Miscellaneous	Right Artillery Trench Mortar Batteries.	23/07/1917	23/07/1917
Miscellaneous	Trench Mortars. Right Artillery Bombardment Programme.	24/07/1917	24/07/1917
Miscellaneous	Right Artillery Trench Mortar Batteries.	25/07/1917	25/07/1917
Miscellaneous	Right Artillery Trench Mortar Batteries.	26/07/1917	26/07/1917
Miscellaneous	Right Artillery Trench Mortar Batteries.	27/07/1917	27/07/1917
Operation(al) Order(s)	38th Divisional Trench Mortar Batteries. Operation Order No. 5	29/07/1917	29/07/1917
Heading	Bombardment Reports 15-31 July 1917		

Miscellaneous	Report On Days Bombardment	15/01/1917	15/01/1917
Miscellaneous	Bombardment Report	16/07/1917	16/07/1917
Miscellaneous	Bombardment Report	17/07/1917	17/07/1917
Miscellaneous	Bombardment Report	13/07/1917	13/07/1917
Miscellaneous	Bombardment Report	18/07/1917	18/07/1917
Miscellaneous	Bombardment Report	19/07/1917	19/07/1917
Miscellaneous	Bombardment Report	20/07/1917	20/07/1917
Miscellaneous	Bombardment Report	21/07/1917	21/07/1917
Miscellaneous		22/07/1917	22/07/1917
Miscellaneous	Bombardment Report	22/07/1917	22/07/1917
Miscellaneous	Right Artillery Trench Mortar Batteries. Bombardment Report.	23/07/1917	23/07/1917
Miscellaneous	Right Artillery Trench Mortar Batteries. Bombardment Report.	25/07/1917	25/07/1917
Miscellaneous	Right Artillery Trench Mortar Batteries. Bombardment Report.	26/07/1917	26/07/1917
Miscellaneous	Right Artillery Trench Mortar Batteries. Bombardment Report.	29/07/1917	29/07/1917
Miscellaneous	Intelligence Summary Right Group 38th. D.A.	30/06/1917	30/06/1917
Miscellaneous	D.T.M.O. 38th Division.	24/08/1917	24/08/1917
Heading	38th Divisional T. M. Batteries August 1917. Vol 14		
War Diary	A17a9.1 Sheet 28 N.W.	01/08/1917	06/08/1917
War Diary	X29.c.7.1. Sheet 19	08/08/1917	18/08/1917
War Diary	X30.d.9.2.Sheet 19	18/08/1917	31/08/1917
Miscellaneous	Right Artillery. Instruction No. 1	07/08/1917	07/08/1917
Heading	Appendix II		
Miscellaneous	A Form. Messages And Signals		
Miscellaneous	Appendix III		
War Diary	Stroud Camp X30d.9.2. Sheet 19	02/09/1917	17/09/1917
War Diary	Camp H9c4.6 Sheet 36	19/09/1917	30/09/1917
Heading	38th Divisional T.M. Batteries October 1917 Vol 16		
War Diary	Birdcage Farm H9c4.6 France Sheet 36	01/10/1917	31/10/1917
Heading	38th Divisional T. M. Batteries November 1917. Vol 17		
War Diary	Birdcage Fm H9c4.6 France Sheet 36	01/11/1917	05/11/1917
War Diary	Birdcage F.M.E H9.c.4.6	05/11/1917	09/11/1917
War Diary	Birdcage Farm H9c.4.6. France Sht. 36	09/11/1917	30/11/1917
Miscellaneous	O.C., Right Group.		
Miscellaneous	38/th. Div. Arty.	25/11/1917	25/11/1917
Heading	Appendix 1 Appendix 2 38th Div TMB War Diary Nov. 1917		
Miscellaneous	115 Infantry Brigade.	01/11/1917	01/11/1917
Miscellaneous	O.C. X/38/T.M.B. Appendix 2	06/11/1917	06/11/1917
Operation(al) Order(s)	Left Group-38th Div. Artillery. Operation Order No. 3	06/11/1917	06/11/1917
Heading	Appendix 3 (a & b) 38th Divnl TMB War Diary Nov. 1917		
Operation(al) Order(s)	Centre Group 38th Divisional Artillery Operation Order No. 29	07/11/1917	07/11/1917
Diagram etc			
Heading	Appendix 4 38th Divnl TMB. War Diary Nov 1917		
Miscellaneous	38th. Divisional Trench Mortar Batteries.		
Miscellaneous	Lines of Fire for "S.O.S." Will be as Follows	27/11/1917	27/11/1917
Miscellaneous	38th Divisional Trench Mortar Batteries.	21/11/1917	21/11/1917
Miscellaneous	Lines of Fire for "S.O.S." Will be as Follows	21/11/1917	21/11/1917
Heading	December 1917 38th Divisional TMB War Diary Vol 18		
War Diary	Birdcage Fm H9c4.6 France Sheet 36	01/12/1917	31/12/1917

Heading	January 1918 38th Divisional TMB War Diary Vol 19		
War Diary	Birdcage Fm H9c.4.6. France Sheet 36	01/01/1918	14/01/1918
War Diary	Birdcage Farm H9c.4.6	16/01/1918	16/01/1918
War Diary	Haverskerque J.34.c.8.7	17/01/1918	17/01/1918
War Diary	J.34.c.8.7	19/01/1918	31/01/1918
Heading	Situation At End Of Month. 38th Division T.M.B. Batteries Engaged In Divisional Training.		
Heading	February 1918. 38th Divisional T.M.B. War Diary Vol 20		
War Diary	Haverskerque J.34.c.8.7	01/02/1918	14/02/1918
War Diary	Erquinghem H.4.c.3.3	17/02/1918	25/02/1918
War Diary	Erquinghem H.4.c.3.3	27/02/1918	27/02/1918
War Diary	Erquinghem H.4.c.3.3	26/02/1918	28/02/1918
Miscellaneous	S.O.S. Orders Left Group Medium Trench Mortars.	28/02/1918	28/02/1918
Miscellaneous	S.O.S. Orders Right Group Medium Trench Mortars.	25/02/1918	25/02/1918
Miscellaneous	S.O.S. Orders Right Group Medium Trench Mortars.		
Heading	38th. Div. T. M. Batteries March 1918 Vol 21		
War Diary	Erquinghem H.4.c.3.3	01/03/1918	30/03/1918
War Diary	Erquinghem H.4.c.3.3	14/03/1918	24/03/1918
War Diary	Erquinghem H.4.c.3.3	21/03/1918	22/03/1918
Heading	V. Corps. Third Army. War Diary 38th Divisional Trench Mortar Batteries. April 1918		
War Diary	Erquinghem	01/04/1918	09/04/1918
War Diary	Steenwerck	10/04/1918	10/04/1918
War Diary	Outersteene	11/04/1918	11/04/1918
War Diary	Le Souverain	12/04/1918	12/04/1918
War Diary	Godewaersvelde	13/04/1918	24/04/1918
War Diary	L 10 (Sh. 27)	25/04/1918	29/04/1918
Miscellaneous	C.29.c.80.20	25/02/1918	25/02/1918
War Diary	St. Janter Beizen.	02/05/1918	20/05/1918
War Diary	Gezaincourt	20/05/1918	29/05/1918
War Diary	Rainecheval	31/05/1918	31/05/1918
Heading	38th (Welsh) Divisional Trench Mortar Batteries June 1918. Vol 24		
War Diary	Gezaincourt Raincheval	01/06/1918	04/06/1918
War Diary	Varennes	05/06/1918	06/06/1918
War Diary	Mesnil	07/06/1918	26/06/1918
War Diary	Work Of	26/06/1918	29/06/1918
Miscellaneous	General		
Miscellaneous	Reference Map Sheet France 5/d SE.		
War Diary	Casualties	04/06/1918	28/06/1918
Heading	War Diary July 1918 38th Divisional Trench Mortar Battalion Vol 25		
War Diary	Varennes	01/07/1918	01/07/1918
War Diary	Mesnil	01/07/1918	30/07/1918
War Diary	Varennes Herissart	31/07/1918	31/07/1918
War Diary	Casualties	06/07/1918	19/07/1918
Heading	War Diary August 1918 38th Divisional Trench Mortar Batteries Vol 26		
War Diary	Senlis	14/08/1918	20/08/1918
War Diary	Martinsart	14/08/1918	20/08/1918
War Diary	Bouzincourt	14/08/1918	20/08/1918
War Diary	Mesnil	14/08/1918	20/08/1918
War Diary	Herissart	01/08/1918	02/08/1918
War Diary	Varennes	06/08/1918	06/08/1918
War Diary	Hedauville	07/08/1918	07/08/1918

Heading	Z 37 T M Bty Vol 1 Apr 16 May 16		
War Diary	Varennes	06/08/1918	31/08/1918
Miscellaneous	Reference Map Sheet France 57 D SE		
War Diary	Sheet 57 D.S.E. & 57 C	22/08/1918	31/08/1918
War Diary	Casualties	01/08/1918	24/08/1918
Heading	War Diary-September 1918 38th Divisional Trench Mortar Batteries. Vol 27		
War Diary	Mametz	01/09/1918	01/09/1918
War Diary	Longueval Morval Manancourt	02/09/1918	06/09/1918
War Diary	Le Sars	07/09/1916	07/09/1916
War Diary	Rocquigny	10/09/1918	10/09/1918
War Diary	Bus	11/09/1918	12/09/1918
War Diary	Equancourt	13/09/1918	17/09/1918
War Diary	Gouzecourt Sector	18/09/1918	18/09/1918
War Diary	Rocquigny (H2 For Gouzeaucourt Sector)	24/09/1918	27/09/1918
War Diary	Equancourt	28/09/1918	30/09/1918
War Diary	Gouzeaucourt Sector	18/09/1918	21/09/1918
War Diary	Rocquigny	22/09/1918	23/09/1918
Miscellaneous	Casualties Appendix I	18/09/1918	18/09/1918
Miscellaneous	Location List. Appendix II (a)		
Miscellaneous	38th Divisional T. M. Batteries. Order No. 1. Appendix II (b)	14/09/1918	14/09/1918
Miscellaneous	38th Divisional Trench Mortar Batteries	14/09/1918	14/09/1918
Operation(al) Order(s)	38th Divisional T. M. Batteries. Operation Order No. 3 Appendix II	17/09/1918	17/09/1918
Operation(al) Order(s)	38th Divl T. M. Batteries Order No. 2 Appendix II b	15/09/1918	15/09/1918
Miscellaneous	Transport Tables	15/09/1918	15/09/1918
Miscellaneous	38th Divisional Trench Mortar Batteries.	15/09/1918	15/09/1918
Miscellaneous	Working Party Table	15/09/1918	15/09/1918
Miscellaneous	Working Party Table	17/09/1918	17/09/1918
Miscellaneous	Location List		
Miscellaneous	Detail of Transport		
Miscellaneous	Working Party Table Appendix III C		
Heading	War Diary October 1918 38 Divisional Trench Mortar Batteries Vol 28		
War Diary	Fins	01/10/1918	04/10/1918
War Diary	Epehy	05/10/1918	14/10/1918
War Diary	Troisvilles	14/10/1918	24/10/1918
War Diary	Croix	25/10/1918	31/10/1918
Miscellaneous	Appendix I		
Heading	November 1918 War Diary Of 38th Divisional T.M. Batteries Vol 29		
War Diary	Croix	01/11/1918	01/11/1918
War Diary	Englefontaine	02/11/1918	06/11/1918
War Diary	Berlaimont	07/11/1918	11/11/1918
War Diary	Aulnoye	11/11/1917	21/11/1917
War Diary	Englefontaine	21/11/1918	30/11/1918
Miscellaneous	Appendix I		
Heading	December 1918 War Diary of 38th Div T.M. Batteries Vol 30		
War Diary	Englefontaine	01/12/1918	28/12/1918
War Diary	Le Quesnoy	28/12/1918	30/12/1918
War Diary	Corbie	30/12/1918	30/12/1918
Heading	January 1919 War Diary 38th Div. T.M. Batteries. Vol 31		
War Diary	Corbie	01/01/1919	02/01/1919

War Diary   Behencourt   02/01/1919   31/01/1919

NORS/2546/17

38TH DIVISION
DIVL ARTILLERY

38TH TRENCH MORTAR BTY

~~APR-MAY 1916~~

1916 APL - 1919 JAN

Index..........................

SUBJECT.

No.	Contents.	Date.

T M B Bart
Bonden
July 1917

WAR DIARY or INTELLIGENCE SUMMARY

Army Form C. 2118.

Z/38 Trench Mortar Battery

Instructions regarding War Diaries and Intelligence Summaries are contained in F.S. Regs., Part II. and the Staff Manual respectively. Title pages will be prepared in manuscript.

Place	Date	Hour	Summary of Events and Information	Remarks and references to Appendices
Ypres	Mar 5th 1916		Z/38 Trench Mortar Battery formed at GORE; and equipped with 1½" Trench mortars.	
"	6, 7, 8th		Fitted drill wooden on guns.	
"	8th		Right section under 2/Lt Schwarz went into the line at Givenchy to be attached X/38 Trench Mortar Battery for instruction.	
"	9th 10th		Left section under Lieut Wilkinson went into the line for instruction. Left resting & drilling on our guns.	
"	11th		2nd line under 2/Lt Wilkinson relieved 1st section, so we were not attached to X/38 T.M.B. for instruction.	
"	12, 13th		Work done to make & improve emplacements. No one getting drilling on guns.	
"	14th		14.50 in show was an aggressive bombardment of the German salient & trenches (Boesinghe) by Trench mortars when the Z/38 fired in medium to retaliate or German whiz-bang.	
"	15th – 8 p.m.		Dull. Work under fire. Every gun & mount into billets 1 p.m.	
"	15		Changed 15 gun for new 2" gun — & mame the	
"	16		Mars of above.	
"	17		Impose to Lain Ctu	

Z 38 T M By
MAY /16
Army Form C. 2118.

X/38 Trench Mortar Battery

WAR DIARY
INTELLIGENCE SUMMARY.
(Erase heading not required.)

Place	Date	Hour	Summary of Events and Information	Remarks and references to Appendices
Fauquissart	1st		Left Estaires relieved X/38 T.M.B. in Fauquissart Sector.	
"	2nd		Battery in Rest	
"	3rd		do	
"	4th		do	
"	5th		do	
"	6th		do	
"	7th		Fatigue parties in the front line	
"	8th		do	
"	9th		do	
"			Battery in support	
"	10th		2/ Lm. Rew. R.F.A. assumed command.	
"	10th		2/ Lt. G.C. Harris R.F.A. landed our, and was transferred to X/38 T.M.B.	
"	11th		Battery in support. Fatigue parties working in the front line	
"	12th		do do	
"	13th		Battery relieved X/38 T.M. Battery in the line	
"	14th 2am.		2 rounds fired at a group of Infantry in retaliation (Fauquissart Right)	
"			5 rounds fired Retaliation (Moated Grange Left).	

T/134. Wt. W708—776. 500000. 4/15. Sir J.C. & E.

WAR DIARY or INTELLIGENCE SUMMARY

Army Form C. 2118.

Z/38 2inch Mortar Battery

Place	Date	Hour	Summary of Events and Information	Remarks and references to Appendices
Laventie	18th		Cleaned guns & assembled them for first time.	
"	19th		Gun drill on own gun.	
"	20th		Lt. --- and 2nd Lt. Harris went into the line with two guns in Fauquissart sector. (normal)	
"	21st		Built & improved gun emplacements. (normal)	
"	22nd		Registered 2 guns. Brought 3rd gun into trenches. (normal. Enemy shelled Shet 16.)	
"	23rd		Registered 3rd gun. Built & improved gun emplacements. (4)	
"	24th		2nd Lt. Shannon relieved Lt. --- & 2nd Lt. Harris.	
"			More work done on gun emplacements. Rt. gun brought into ln. 16	
"	25th		Fire on enemy salient, Sugar Loaf (normal. some hostile shelling.)	
"	26th		1st Lt. B.G.? Bee Major inspected work done on emplacements etc.	
"			2nd Lt. Shannon went on telephone course. 2nd Lt. Harris relieved him in lin.	
"			Registered on Sugar Loaf. Work on emplacements proceeded with	
"	27th 28th		2 new guns issued for retaliation. Worked on "	
night of 28/29th			Gun alarm. Fired 9 rounds. Direct hit on enemy parapet at 3 a.m.	
"			Retaliation on gun emplacements & Rotten Row was heavy.	
"	30th		2nd Lt. Harris relieved by 2nd Lt. Shannon. Work proceeded with.	

Army Form C. 2118

WAR DIARY
or
INTELLIGENCE SUMMARY
(Erase heading not required.)

Vol 12

38th Divisional T.M. Batteries.

June 1917

Army Form C. 2118

WAR DIARY
or
INTELLIGENCE SUMMARY
(Erase heading not required.)

Place	Date	Hour	Summary of Events and Information	Remarks and references to Appendices
STEENTJE FARM Camp Sheet 28 A17492	1/7	2.30 pm	Bombardment of CANAL AVENUE trench by heavy T.M. and 2 guns in Left group. gun reported at C7C 15.70	
	2		Bombardment of Enemy Front line by Heavy T.M. at points between C7d 10.70 and C7C 95.75. 35 rounds. Right group medium guns opposite KIEL COT and retaliated for 2 hostile minenwerfers with 19 rounds. Left group bombarded BABOO LANE. Right group medium cut wire for C7a 55.75 C7d 70.95. Fired in retaliation for hostile shelling 50 rounds.	
	3			
	4	3.30 am 5.0 12-0-3.0 pm	Heavy T.M. registration with aeroplane observation. Right group heavies retaliated for hostile minenwerfers 31 rounds. Left group bombarded BABOO LANE firing 200 rounds without any hostile activity.	
	5		Right group bombarded Enemy front line from KIEL COT & FARM 14 and cut wire close C13 6 90.85	

WAR DIARY
or
INTELLIGENCE SUMMARY

Army Form C. 2118

(Erase heading not required.)

Place	Date	Hour	Summary of Events and Information	Remarks and references to Appendices
STEENTJE FARM CAMP Sheet 28 A17 d 9 2	5	3.0 p.m MN 12.0	Left group fired 30 rounds in accordance with T.M. 817 and 80 rounds in conjunction with raid	T.M. 819
	6/7	4.15 pm	Heavy T.M. fired 10 rounds in conjunction with demonstration T.M. 822. Regtl. group fired 62 rounds. 3 men wounded. Left bombards BARBO LANE and fired 68 rounds in retaliation for 6 2 Lieut W.A. JONES R.F.A. reported for duty. Post T & X B/G	T.M. 822
	7/8	10 p.m	Heavy T.M. fires in conjunction with gas operation and left group fired in connection with suspected enemy relief	
	8/9	Mdnt N.O.	Heavy T.M. fires in connection with attempted raid on C7 d 1.6½. Reply from fires 49 rounds on C7 d 1.6½. 27 in conjunction with raid. Left Enemy approached parapet dispersed by 2 Hichon bombs + some firing in retaliation 40 rounds for 1 minenwerfer	
	9	2.0 pm	Retaliation only on Right. Left group bombarded B5d 55.95 2/Lt W.A. JONES and 2 O.R. wounded	
	10		Right 66 rounds fired in connection with O.O. 39. Retaliation only in left sector	O.O.39

WAR DIARY or INTELLIGENCE SUMMARY

Army Form C. 2118

Place	Date	Hour	Summary of Events and Information	Remarks and references to Appendices
STEENTJE FARM Camp Sheet 28 A 17 d 9.2	11		Wincester shoot on C.7.d.8.2. 4 & 9 fm rounds in retaliation. Only retaliation in Left Sector	
	12/14		The T.M. firing was confined to retaliation for hostile minenwerfer 2/Lt H. MUSKER. R.G.A. in Charge of X Bty during Lt HARRIS' leave of absence	
	15	3.0pm	Right group fired in retaliation 15 rounds	
	16		2/Lt C.H. MOORE R.F.A. reported for duty and posted to X Bty	
	17		Preparations for handing over Left Group the BOESINGHE area to the D.T.M.O. 1 Guards Division commenced	
	18			
	19	pm 9.0	BOESINGHE Sector handed over to Guards Divisional T.M's at 9.0 pm	
	21	1/0	Some support by M.T.M's. on raid	
	22		Lt HARRIS resumed command of X Bty	
	23-26		No T.M. activity, all men and detachment employed on construction of emplacements in accordance with programme	
	26		Capt O.J. JONES R.F.A. 360 T.M.O. proceeded on leave to PARIS, Capt L.W. FOX G.L. of D.T.M.O. during his absence	
	28		No T.M. activity. 1 Gunner wounded & 4 O.R. gassed by shell	
	30		Work continued by Batteries in Rs. lines	

E.J. Miller Williamson
Lt RFA G.

WAR DIARY or INTELLIGENCE SUMMARY

Army Form C. 2118

Arty M Afg Vol 13

Place	Date	Hour	Summary of Events and Information	Remarks and references to Appendices
A17a9¼ Sheet 28	1/7/17		1. Capt. L.W. FOX SC. A/DTMO. See last diary 26/6/17. 5. O.R. sent to 2nd Army T.M. School for 6" Newton course (5 days)	
		4.0 pm	Relief of detachments which has been in line for 8 days carried out. Control of work in both groups taken on by 2/Lt HARRIS & 2/Lt BRIGGS	
	2	10 pm	Capt B.J. JONES returns & takes command of T.M's. Lieuts G.F.A. GREY, B.V. CLARK & 2/Lieut E.J. MILLER-WILLIAMS sent on 5 days course in 6" NEWTON T.M. at 2nd Army T.M School	
	2·5		All available men working in lines on emplacements preparation to Bombardment scheme	
	5.	4.0 pm	Relief of detachment which has been in line for 6 days from Bour. 2 Corporals report from Bour 5 O.R. sent to 2nd Army T.M School for course of 6" NEWTON T.M. under 2/Lt T.F. BRIGGS 20 Dw. T.M's under Capt A MUNRO GLEN R.F.A. report to DTMO 38 for bombardment scheme 6. Dw. T.M.'s under Capt WEBB report to 36 DTMO	
	6.		During the period no rounds were fired, no T.M activity by enemy	

WAR DIARY or INTELLIGENCE SUMMARY

Army Form C. 2118

Place	Date	Hour	Summary of Events and Information	Remarks and references to Appendices
A17a9.1	7	7	15 Rounds fired in retaliation for 3 LOTTM Minenwerfer 1 man wounded.	
Sheet 28 NW	8	12.30pm – 2.40	50 Rounds fired by Right Group 25 by Left in retaliation 2 men wounded	
	9		Instructions No 1 issued to Groups to retaliate for 1 LOTTM TM with 5. Right Group retaliated	TM 858.
			Right Group retaliated with 16 rounds for Hostile shelling + a few Minenwerfer	
	11/12	3.30 AM	10 Rounds fired in neighbourhood of FARM 14 – Retaliation	
	12-14		All energies on ammunition supply + improvements in the line 2 wounded	
C19a 0.3	14		Orgns for Bombardment issued, also O.O. No 1 issued	TM 862.
Sheet 28 NW	15	12.0 Noon	D.T.M.O moves H.Q. into the line, & C19 a 0.3	TM OO No 1
		6–9pm	Bombardment commences Right Group fires on C136 40 to 80 & C14a 00.70	
		10–12	Also C13 b 90.72 a small patch of wire remain also on Top of CAESAR's NOSE	
		6–10	Left Group bombard trench C7d 55–60 & C7d 40 65. Heavy Group bombard CACTUS POINT 10 rounds. There was no enemy retaliation	
	16	6.0 AM 10.0 10.30 AM 12.30pm	Right Group bombard (1) Communication trench C 14a 10.65 & C14 a 25–70 (2) C 14a 20.30 to C14a 35.20 (3) C 7d 50.60 & C 7d 50.30 } Wire largely cleared. 2 men wounded.	
		10.30 AM 12.35pm	One premature occurred but no one was injured	

WAR DIARY
or
INTELLIGENCE SUMMARY
(Erase heading not required.)

Army Form C. 2118

Instructions regarding War Diaries and Intelligence Summaries are contained in F. S. Regs., Part II. and the Staff Manual respectively. Title Pages will be prepared in manuscript.

Place	Date	Hour	Summary of Events and Information	Remarks and references to Appendices
C.19.a.0.3	16/11	7.0 a.m.	Lift groups engaged (1) C.7.d.10.70 to C.7.d.40.65	See details reports appended.
			(2) C.7.c.40.75 to C.7.c.40.57 } No retaliation	
		10-11.0 a.m.	(3) C.7.c.40.57 to C.7.c.90.73 } Great damage done	
		10-11.45 a.m.	Heavy group engaged C.7.d.10.70	
	17	9-11 a.m.	The following targets were engaged by Right group Wire C.7.d.75.55 to C.7.d.80.30	
		9-11.30 a.m.	Wire opposite FINCH COTTAGE - Slight enemy retaliation 77 m.m. gun	
		9-12.30 a.m.	Wire from C.7.d.75.65 to C.7.d.80.30	
			By Left Group.	
		5-8.0 a.m.	Wire at MOUND	
		8-12.30	Wire C.7.c.75.75 to C.7.c.95.75 } Results very effective	
		10-12.30 a.m.	Wire C.7.d.40.65 & KIEL COT	
			By Heavy group.	
		6-8.30 a.m.	C.7.d.10.70 } Both 9.45 & 6" Newton fires	
		10-12 noon	& KIEL COT area	
		2-5 p.m.	Much trouble experienced by communication lines cut by hostile shelling. Heavy fire on MOUND 40 rounds.	

Army Form C. 2118

WAR DIARY
or
INTELLIGENCE SUMMARY

(Erase heading not required.)

Instructions regarding War Diaries and Intelligence Summaries are contained in F. S. Regs., Part II. and the Staff Manual respectively. Title Pages will be prepared in manuscript.

Place	Date	Hour	Summary of Events and Information	Remarks and references to Appendices
C19a 0.3	18.7.17	6-9pm	Rgtl Group engaged. C14a 90·75 & FAASH COT.	See separate detailed reports.
		11-12.30 AM PM	Wire C14a 35-40 & C14a 40·22	
		7-11 AM	" C7a 95·20 & C13b 98·95	
		6-11	" C14a 90·75 & FLASH COT	
		5-11	" C7d 95·20 & C13b 98·98	
	11/12 MNT		In response to S.O.S. 20 Rounds fired on CAESARS NOSE	
			Left Group	
		6-2 AM	Turned C7d 20·70 & C7d 40·70.	
		6-11 AM	" C7c 30·90 & C7c 40·90	
		10-12.30 AM	" C7c 70·80 & C7d 60·80.	
		9-11	Heavy trench mortar 10 rounds 20	
			the MOUND the PIMPLE – C14a 10·95	
		9.30AM 12.30 PM	6" NEWTON C14a 0·7 & FLASH COT.	
			C7d 70·60 & C7d 80·40.	
		6-7 pm	Very successful shoot much damage done. Target the MOUND 140 Rounds cullet rendle	
		11.30 pm	Heavy fire 3 rounds C7d 10·70 in response to S.O.S	

WAR DIARY
or
INTELLIGENCE SUMMARY
(Erase heading not required.)

Army Form C. 2118

Instructions regarding War Diaries and Intelligence Summaries are contained in F. S. Regs., Part II. and the Staff Manual respectively. Title Pages will be prepared in manuscript.

Place	Date	Hour	Summary of Events and Information	Remarks and references to Appendices
C19 a 0.3	19	6-12.30 am pm	Right Group fired on Targets. C13b 80·80 to C7d 96·95. C14a 20·55 to C14a 30·40. 9·50 Rounds retaliation. C7a 85·36 to C7d 95·20. One man wounded.	See the detailed reports of programme
		"	Left Group. C7c 75·75 to C7d 10·70. C7d 10·70 to C7d 55·60.	
		11-Am 12-0 pm	Heavy Group. The MOUND. Point 7 CAESARS NOSE. CACTUS JUNCTION C7d 70·50. KIEL COT.	
	20	6-2·0 pm		
		6-Ar	Right Group fired on. FLASH COT to C14c 30·40. CAESARS NOSE DUGOUTS. C7d 60·40 to C7d 90·20	
		12.30 pm	Left Group. C7c 45·90. C7e 72·80. C7d 07·70. C7d 35·69. C7c 56·78. CX 32·90.	
		2-5pm 8-12 hrs	Heavy group fired on CABLE & CACTUS Junction. 2 Short rounds in our line. The PIMPLE. C14a 30·40 to C14a 45·15. Retaliation by 10cm guns. C7d 75·60 to C7d 50·40. C7c 98·95 + Dugouts round CACTUS Junction	
	21	2-5pm 9-11 Am	Right Group fired on C7d 45·65 to C7d 75·50. C8c 05·00 to C8a 20·75. C14a 31·41 to C14a 13·60.	

WAR DIARY or INTELLIGENCE SUMMARY

Army Form C. 2118

(Erase heading not required.)

Place	Date	Hour	Summary of Events and Information	Remarks and references to Appendices
C19a 0.3	21/17	6-12 noon	Left group fired on C7c 32 90 & C7c 55 75 C7d 95 75 to C7d 05 65	Dugout destroyed at C7d 80 65. See type reports & programmes
			Heavy group: C14a 25 95 to C8d 10 10. e 63 52 — Minimum range e 7b 30 90 could not be C7e 95 75 C7c 30 75 & C7c 30 90 V very good results C7d 95 70	
	22	8-12	Right group fired on C7d 45 55 to C7d 75 50 C14a 47 17 & C14a 31 41 1 Prisoner - no casualties C14a 10 95 & C14a 20 70 LIEUT EDELL 26, wounded.	
		7-2.0pm	Left group fired on C7c 56 78 & C7c 85 78 C7e 32 90 & C7c 58 78 C7d 15 70 (WW) 1 bn destroyed by enemy shell fire. C7c 32 90 & C7c 58 78	
		10.30am	Heavy group Target C7c 95 80 to C7c 75 80 C7c 60 75 & C7c 71 80 C7d 30 70 & C7a 40 60 C14c 20 85 & C8c 10 65 Dugouts.	
		12.30pm		
	23	10 am	Right group target C14a 30 90 & C14a 45 15 C8c 10 25 & C14a 10 95 C7d 40 55 & C7d 75 50	
		7 am -12.30 pm	Left group target C7c 5 7 & C7c 6 7 C7d 87 & C7a 37 C7c 67 & C7c 67 Heavy enemy retaliation	
		2.0pm		

Army Form C. 2118

WAR DIARY
or
INTELLIGENCE SUMMARY

(Erase heading not required.)

Instructions regarding War Diaries and Intelligence Summaries are contained in F. S. Regs., Part II. and the Staff Manual respectively. Title Pages will be prepared in manuscript.

Place	Date	Hour	Summary of Events and Information	Remarks and references to Appendices
C.19.a.0.3	23/24	9.0 p.m – 12.0 noon	Heavy group targets C.7.d.15.85 C.7.c.95.75 – C.7.c.90.80 Mortar damaged by shell fire C.7.d.50.60 C.14.a.25.85 C.8.c.25.25 Target obliterated C.8.c.10.00 C.8.c.15.25	
	23/24		Lieut B.V. CLARK to hospital sick. Canal bank heavily shelled with gas shelling, approx 9 men gassed.	
	24	9.0 a.m 12.30 p.m	Right group. Lapts Trenches C.14.a.30.40 C.14.a.15.20 C.14.a.25.80 C.14.a.45.65. Heavy retaliation C.7.d.85.60 C.8.c.05.30	
		8–11 a.m	Left group fired on trenches C.7.c.32.90 C.7.c.56.78. C.7.d.30.40	
		9–12 hrs	Heavy group fired on MAUSER COT. NEST at C.7.d.18.68 Visibility poor CACTUS POINT	
			1 Man to hospital gassed.	
	25	11.0 a.m – 3.0 p.m	Right group targets C.7.d.75.55 – C.7.d.90.25 C.14.a.60.60	
		5–7 p.m	Left group targets B.12.d.97.90 B.12.d.97.90 – C.7.c.12.90	
		12–hrs 2.0 p.m	Heavy group MAUSER COT. C.8.c.15.25 B.12.d.96.80 – C.7.c.10.95. Observation poor Trouble with telephone wires being continually cut.	
			One man wounded.	

WAR DIARY
or
INTELLIGENCE SUMMARY
(Erase heading not required.)

Army Form C. 2118

Instructions regarding War Diaries and Intelligence Summaries are contained in F.S. Regs., Part II. and the Staff Manual respectively. Title Pages will be prepared in manuscript.

Place	Date	Hour	Summary of Events and Information	Remarks and references to Appendices
C19 a 0.3 Sheet 28 NW	26/11	3-6pm	Right group fired on C14 a 35-55 & C14 a 50.15. Heavy retaliation. Left Group fired on The MOUND. 14 rounds only Heavy. Unobserved. C8 c 80.40 MAUSER COT. C14 a 55.65 C8 c 20.25	See Schedule report & programme
	27/11	10-11 AM	Right group fired on front line & MOUND C7c 25.95 4 rounds all communications cut.	
		8-10 AM	Left group fired on wire in front of MOUND. One man wounded	
	28	10-12 noon	Right group fired on CAESARS RESERVE & SUPPORT CACTUS JUNCTION & POINT.	
		6-9:30	Heavy group fired on dump on Canal bank being blown up by enemy. 2 men killed	
	29	6-12 noon	Right group fired in burst of fire on CAESARS SUPPORT & RESERVE and on KIEL COT Heavy group engaged CACTUS RESERVE CADDIE RESERVE CADDIE POINT and GALLWITZ FARM. Heavy retaliation During the period 25/29 11 the enemy shelled CANAL bank with gas all night.	

WAR DIARY or INTELLIGENCE SUMMARY

Army Form C. 2118

Place	Date	Hour	Summary of Events and Information	Remarks and references to Appendices
C.19.a.0.3	30/17	10-12 noon	Heavy group fire on CACTUS JUNCTION area & C.9.c.15.40 in bunds of fire with 8m in bursts.	
		2 pm	All Batteries save X & 2/38 withdrawn from the line to billets. 1st G.S. HARRIS taken command 7.2/38	
A.17.a.9.1	31	noon	ZERO DAY. T.M's did not fire. D.T.M.O. moves H.Q from the line to A 17 a 9.1. Sheet 26 NW Division required 110 mm for stretcher bearers. 40 of these were supplied by this unit.	

			Appendices I Bombardment Instruction
			                  II Bombardment Programme
			                  III Bombardment Report	

E.J. Miller Williams
2 Lt R.F.R.G.

38 Divisional T.M.
Instructions
July 1917

I

T.M. 856.

38th DIVISIONAL TRENCH MORTAR BATTERIES.

INSTRUCTIONS NO. 1.
---oOo---

ORGANIZATION.

T.M. Batteries in the line will be organized into the following three Groups.
1. Heavy T.M. Group composed of V/38/T.M.B., V/20/T.M.B., and Z/38/T.M.B. (armed with three 6" Newton T.Ms.), under command of Captain L.W. FOX., M.C., V/38/T.M.B.
2. Right Medium T.M. Group composed of X/38/T.M.B., Z/20/T.M.B and Z/61/T.M.B. under command of Lieut. G.G. HARRIS., M.C., R.F.A.
3. Left Medium T.M. Group composed of Y/38/T.M.B., X/20/T.M.B and Y/20/T.M.B. under command of Captain Glen., R.F.A.

LOCATIONS AND DISTRIBUTION OF WORK.

Heavy T.M. Group.
V/38/T.M.B.- Work on 4 emplacements in WEST CANAL BANK.
V/20/T.M.B.- Work on 3 emplacements in FARGATE and one emplacement in WEST CANAL BANK at C.13.c.1.6., with assistance from V/38/T.M.B.
Z/38/T.M.B.- Work on 3 emplacements in FARGATE.

Right M.T.M. Group.
X/38/T.M.B.- Work on 4 emplacements in BULLY TRENCH.
Z/61/T.M.B.- Work on 4 emplacements in POST 24.
Z/20/T.M.B.- Work on 2 emplacements in HUDDLESTON TRENCH and 2 emplacements in INKERMAN TRENCH.

Left M.T.M. Group.
Y/20/T.M.B.- Work on 4 emplacements in ALMA TRENCH.
X/20/T.M.B.- Work on 4 emplacements in HARWICH TRENCH.
Y/38/T.M.B.- Work on 4 emplacements near BAIRD TRENCH.

LOCATION OF PERSONNEL.

Until accommodation is built at Battery positions, personnel of 38th Div. T.M.Bs. will live on WEST CANAL BANK in C.13.c. personnel of 20th Div. T.M.Bs. and Z/61/T.M.B. will live in copse in B.23.d. Remainder of personnel of 61st Div. T.M.Bs. will be in reserve at A.17.a.8.2.

D.T.M.O. 61st Division will supply the following working parties :-
A. Party of 2 Officers and 17 men to work at T.M. Dump MARENGO HOUSE.
B. Party of one Officer and 15 men to work on D.T.M.O's H.Q. at C.19.a.0.5.
C. Party of one Officer and 50 men to load lorries at Divisional Bomb Store. Details to be arranged daily.

T.M.856/3.

38th DIVISIONAL TRENCH MORTAR BATTERIES.

AMMUNITION SUPPLY.

Reference T.M. 856/2, Ammunition Supply.
Party "A" will in future be composed as follows :-

1. 100 men of the HAMPSHIRE Regt. to report at MARENGO HOUSE at 8-0 am to Right M.T.M.Group Ammunition Officer for the purpose of carrying ammunition up to the emplacements by hand.

2. 100 men of the MIDDLESEX Regt. to report at MARENGO HOUSE at 9-0 am to Left M.T.M.Group Ammunition Officer for the purpose of carrying ammunition up to emplacements by hand.

These parties are entirely under the control of the Group Ammunition Officers. They must be used mainly for carrying ammunition from the RESERVE DUGOUTS forward, and only when absolutely necessary should portions of them be used for mopping up. Each Group Ammunition Officer should have at least one N.C.O. and 5 Guides to aid him in controlling the party. On no account must the party be left at the mercy of a N.C.O.

These parties are detailed to report to the D.T.M.O. at MARENGO HOUSE. Officers meeting the parties will keep this in mind. The D.T.M.O. will not be there.

The Heavy T.M. Group will not have any day parties in future unless special application is made to D.T.M.O. 61st Division.

Captain R.F.A.
D.T.M.O. 38th Division.

10-7-17.

T.M.835/2.

38th DIVISIONAL TRENCH MORTAR BATTERIES.

ADDENDA TO T.M. INSTRUCTIONS NO. 14

1. AMMUNITION SUPPLY.

   a. Serial numbers of Infantry carrying parties are now as follows -

Serial No. of party.	Strength.	To report at T.M. Dump at.	Work.
A.	50	6-0 am	To carry Heavy T.M. ammunition by hand, and to collect any H.T.M. ammunition lying about the trenches. This party will be entirely at disposal of H.T.M. Group ammunition Officer.
B	150 (in 3 sections of 50)	10-30 pm	To push trucks. One section per Group.
C	50	10-30 pm	To distribute ammunition from Right M.T.M. Group Dump to emplacements. To be met and controlled by Group ammunition Officer.
D	50	10-30 pm	To work in Left M.T.M. Group as in "C"
E	100	10-30 pm	To work in Heavy T.M. Group as in "C" and "D".
F	50	10-30 pm	To work at T.M. Dump, to unload lorries and to mop up H.T.M. ammunition lying about tramways.

   b. A new T.M. dump is being formed at E.24.c.1.1. From the 10th inst. inclusive ammunition and all rations will be dumped at the new dump. Ammunition remaining at the present dump near MARENGO HOUSE will be treated as a reserve, to be issued by O.C. T.M. Dump only when Infantry parties cannot be supplied from the new dump.
   O.C. T.M. Dump will leave 2 storemen in charge at the old dump. Material will continue to be dumped at the old dump. Each Group will be notified as to the amount of material arriving for it at nightly. Groups will arrange parties to unload their own material.

2. REPORTS.

   O.C. T.M. Dump will render daily, at his earliest convenience, a detailed report on the working of Infantry parties during the previous night.
   Group Commanders are reminded that reports must arrive at this Office punctually as possible at 10-0 am. Otherwise considerable disorganisation will ensue.

O J Jones

Captain R.F.A.
D.T.M.O. 38th Division.

10-7-17.

AMMUNITION SUPPLY.

A. TRANSPORT.

Available lorries will report to Div. Bomb Store at 8-0 pm daily. To be loaded up by party from 61st Div T.M.Bs. Lorries will proceed to T.M. Dump near MARENGO HOUSE, C.19.c.0.6 Two journeys will be made if possible.

B. T.M. DUMP.

Control of the Dump will be taken over by Lieut. E.W.N. MAY., R.F.A., 61st T.M.Bs. 2/Lieut J.V. COLLINS R.F.A. will assist Lieut. MAY until further notice.

30 trucks will be placed at his disposal every night by O. i/c Trench Tramways 29th Division, who must be consulted daily with regard to the supply of trucks.

O.C. T.M. Dump will take charge of all material brought up th the dump for issue to T.M. Groups. This material will be earmarked for the different Groups before arrival at the Dump.

C. GROUP RESERVE DUMPS.

Each T.M. Group Commander will select a position near the terminus of the trench tramway which supplies his Group where ammunition can be dumped pending distribution to emplacem-ments. Narrow trenches will be dug at these dumps as soon as possible. An Officer will be appointed in each Group to supervise the supply of ammunition to his Group. This Officer will report to the O. i/c T.M. Dump. at 10-0 pm nightly with 1 N.C.O. and 1 man to act as guides to the Infantry parties allotted to Groups.

D. INFANTRY CARRYING PARTIES. Total 450 men daily.

Serial No. of Party.	Strength.	To report at T.M.Dump at.	Work.
A.	50	6-0 am	To carry Heavy T.M. ammunition by hand, and to collect any H.T.M. ammunition lying about the trenches. This party will be entirely at disposal of H.T.M. Group ammunition Officer.
B	50	10-30 pm	To work at T.M. Dump, to unload lorries, and to mop up M.T.M. ammun--ition lying about tramways.
C	150 (in 3 sections of 50)	10-30 pm	To push trucks. One section per Group.
D	50	10-30 pm	To distribute ammunition from Right M.T.M. Group Dump to emplacements. To be met and controlled by Group ammunition Officer.
E	50	10-30 pm	To work in Left M.T.M.Group as in "D"
F	100	10-30 pm	To work in Heavy T.M. Group as in "D" and "E"

NOTE.

a. Each party will know its serial number and will be referred to by that number.

b. Parties "E" and "F" will arrive in lorries at Cross Roads in B.30.a. where they will be met by guides from T.M. Dump. They will proceed to the Dump across the fields, ten minutes interval between parties, parties in alphabetical order.

c. In case of a serious breakdown of any trench tramway delaying any one section of party "C", the section will proceed to carry the ammunition by hand to the Group Reserve Dump. Also, as regards parties "D", "E", and "F" - if no ammunition is available at Group Reserve Dump, and if any extraordinary delay occurs in the arrival of

Party "C" at terminus of tramline, the party concerned will return along tramline and will proceed to carry by hand.

d. GUIDES. In addition to the guides brought by Group Ammunition Officers for Parties "D", "E", and "F", The following extra guides will be supplied from each Group for its section of party "C" :- One N.C.O. and one man. Heavy T.M. Group ammunition Officer will increase the number of his guides when carrying ammunition by hand to FARGATE positions. Guides to report at TM Dump ½ an hour before parties are due.

RATION SUPPLY.

For Batteries on CANAL BANK to be delivered at T.M. Dump.

For Batteries in B.23.d. to be delivered at B.23.d.7.6.

Acknowledge

8-7-17.

O J Jones
Captain R.F.A.
D.T.M.O. 38th Division.

38th DIVISIONAL TRENCH MORTAR BATTERIES.

INSTRUCTIONS No. 2.

1. HEADQUARTERS STAFF.

   On the night of the 14th inst. D.T.M.O. 38th Division. will establish his H.Q. on West Canal Bank, C.19.a.0.6.

   D.T.M.Os. staff will be composed as follows :-

Adjutant	2/Lieut E.J.MILLER-WILLIAMS R.F.A.
a/B.S.M.	Sergt. F.APPLEYARD V/38/T.M.B.
Clerks	Corpl. G.E.JONES V/38/T.M.B.
	Gunner MORTON V/38/T.M.B.
Signallers	Gunner CRITCHLEY V/38/T.M.B.
	2 Signallers from 20th Div. T.M.Bs.
	2 Signallers from 61st Div. T.M.Bs
Linesmen	Gunner CORCORAN Z/38/T.M.B.
	1 Linesman from 20th Div. T.M.Bs.
Orderlies	2 Orderlies from each T.M.Group
	1 Orderly from O.C. T.M. Dump.
	2 Orderlies from D.T.M.O. 61st Div
H.Q. Orderlies	Gunner COOMBES V/38/T.M.B.
	Gunner PEACOCK Z/38/T.M.B.
Cook	1 Cook from 61st Div. T.M.Bs.
Ration and Sanitary Orderly	Gunner P. JONES Y/38/T.M.B.
Batmen	Gunner WATKINS V/38/T.M.B.
	Gunner BATLEY Y/38/T.M.B.

2. Signallers appointed by 20th D.T.M.O. and 61st D.T.M.O. must be experienced men Orderlies must be specially selected for the work needed.

3. The above personnel will rendezvous at T.M. Camp at 10-0 am on the 14th inst.

4. T. M. POOL.

   The T.M. POOL will be formed at T.M. Camp A.17.a.9.1.

   1. The following personnel will be available at this pool :-
      - Details 38th Div. T.M.Bs.   See appendix "A"
      - Details 20th Div. T.M.Bs.   See appendix "B"
      - Details 61st Div. T.M.Bs.   See appendix "C"

   11. The following guns will be held at this pool :-
2" T.Ms.	Z/38/T.M.B.	4
2" T.Ms.	X/61/T.M.B.	4
2" T.Ms.	Y/38/T.M.B.	4
	Total	12

   111. The following transport will be available for ration supply :-
        - 2 G.S. Wagons)
        - 4 Teams   ) Attached from D.A.C. 38th Div.

   1V. D.T.M.O. 61st Division will take over command of this POOL and will be responsible for
       a. Supply of ammunition and supplies to the line.
       b. Supply of Ordnance stores to 38th, 20th, and 61st T.M.Bs, in conjunction with Acting Q.M.S's 38th and 20 th T.M.Bs.

   He will work in direct communication with D.T.M.O. 38th Division, O.C. T.M. Dump, and if necessary direct with 38th Div. Arty.

13-7-17.

Captain R.F.A.
D.T.M.O. 38th Division.

INSTRUCTIONS No. 2.

APPENDIX "A"

Details of 38th Div. T.M.Bs. will be composed as follows :-

Acting Q.M.S.	Corporal WALMSLEY	V/38/T.M.B.
Cook	Gunner WINSTANLEY	V/38/T.M.B.
Groom	Driver J. GWILT	V/38/T.M.B.
Transport	8 O.R. attached from D.A.C.	
Storemen etc.	Gunner PRICE	V/38/T.M.B.
	Gunner RANSON	V/38/T.M.B.
	Gunner ROWLES	V/38/T.M.B.
	Gunner ROSE	V/38/T.M.B.

APPENDIX "B"

Details of 20th Div. T.M.Bs. will be composed as follows :-

?.

APPENDIX "C"

Details of 61st Div. T.M.Bs. will be composed as follows :-

?.

Bombardment
Programme
July 1917.

II

T.M. 854.

36th DIVISIONAL TRENCH MORTAR BATTERIES.

ORDERS FOR THE RELIEFS 6-7-16.

Detachments of Batteries in billets will relieve the
detachments which have been in the line for eight days.

Reliefs will leave billets at 4-0 pm.

5-7-16.

2/Lieut. R.A. for
Captain
D.T.M.O. 36th Division.

"A" Form. Army Form C. 2121.
MESSAGES AND SIGNALS. No. of Message............

Prefix........Code........m	Words	Charge	This message is on a/c of :	Recd. at............m
Office of Origin and Service Instructions.	Sent		................Service.	Date............
	At......m			From............
	To........			
	By........		(Signature of "Franking Officer.")	By............

TO {

| Sender's Number | Day of Month | In reply to Number | |
| M853 | 1-7-17 | | A A A |

Relief will take place tomorrow as follows:-

A'' detachment will relieve detachment which have been in the line for 8 days.

Lieut Hearne will hand over entire & command to both parties to 2/4 R.F.A(T)

Relief will move off at 4-7 pm

2/1 RFA(T)
for Col. Comdg.

From
Place   Kingsdown
Time

The above may be forwarded as now corrected.   (Z)
....
Censor.   Signature of Addressor or person authorised to telegraph in his name.
* This line should be erased if not required.
(A1) O. Ltd., London— W.14042/M.44. 150,000 Pads. 12/15. Form C.2121.

Targets. Trenches. 1. The MOUND.
2. Saps. C.7.c.40.90. and C.7.d.40.65.
3. Group of trenches around junction of CADDIE SUPPORT and KIEL COT.
4. Point of CAESARS NOSE Salient.
5. Communication trench C.14.a.10.70. to C.14.a.25.80.

The 6" Newton Battery will be held in reserve in order to deal daily with the targets which the Medium and Heavy T.Ms. have been unable to engage effectually.

13-7-17.

Captain R.F.A.
D.T.M.O. 36th Division.

RIGHT ARTILLERY TRENCH MORTAR BATTERIES.
OPERATION ORDER No. 2.

---

1. On the 18th inst. Z/20/T.M.B. will move from positions in HUDDLESTON and INKERMAN TRENCHES to relieve Y/38/T.M.B. in positions near BAIRD TRENCH. Y/38/T.M.B. will occupy the positions evacuated by Z/20/T.M.B. On completion of relief, Z/20/T.M.B. will come under control of O.C. Left Medium T.M. Group, and Y/38/T.M.B. under O.C. Right Medium T.M. Group.

II. Relief will commence at 2-0 pm and will be complete by 6-0 pm.

III Mortars in position will be exchanged. Gunstores will not be exchanged.

IV. ACKNOWLEDGE.

18-7-17.

Captain R.F.A.
D.T.M.O. 38th Division.

Copies to :- O.C. Right Medium T.M. Group
O.C. Left Medium T.M. Group
38th Div. Arty.
20th Div. Arty.
D.T.M.O. 61st Division.

T.M. 1/7.

RIGHT ARTILLERY TRENCH MORTAR BATTERIES.
BOMBARDMENT PROGRAMME 19-7-17.

Target	Time	Calibre	No. of guns.
Trench junction C.7.a.50.25	6-0 am to 8-0 am	9.45"	2
Trench around and dugout C.8.c.10.05.	9-30 am to 12-30 pm	9.45"	1
Trenches around KIEL COT	9-0 am to 11-0 am	9.45"	2
THE MOUND	11-0 am to 2-0 pm	9.45"	1
Trenches around C.7.c.58.78.	5-0 pm to 7-0 pm	9.45"	2
Trench C.7.d.75.55. to C.7.d.73.40	8-30 am to 10-0 am	6" NEWTON	1
Trench C.13.b.85.88. to C.13.b.95.75.	11-0 am to 2-0 pm	6" NEWTON	1
Wire at THE MOUND	5-0 pm to 7-0 pm	6" NEWTON	1
Trench C.14.a.20.55. to C.14.a.30.40.	9-30 am to 12-30 pm	2"	4
Trench C.13.b.90.80 to C.7.d.98.05.	9-0 am to 11-0 am	2"	4
Trench C.7.d.05.35. to C.7.d.95.20.	10-30 am to 12-30 pm	2"	4.
(Wire and Trench at the MOUND	6-0 am to 8-0 am	2"	3) X
Wire C.7.c.85.80 to C.7.d.05.62.	8-0 am to 11-0 am	2"	3
Wire C.7.d.10.70. to C.7.d.55.60.	11-0 am to 12-30 pm	2"	4

O J Jones

18-7-17.

Captain R.F.A.
D.T.M.O. 38th Division.

2 telephones for Ruddles

T.M. 1/4.

RIGHT ARTILLERY TRENCH MORTARS.

BOMBARDMENT SCHEME.   18-7-17.

Task	Time.	Calibre	No. of guns.	
THE MOUND	6-0 am to 11-0 am	9.45"	1	H.1
Trench from C.7.a.40.30. to CACTUS JUNCTION.	5-0 pm to 7-0 pm	9.45"	1	H.3
CAESAR SUPPORT around C.14.a.30.75.	10-30 am to 12-30 pm	9.45" Long	1	L.2
Trench Junction C.7.a.40.30.	5-0 pm to 8-0 pm	9.45"	1	H.4
Trench and wire around THE MOUND	5-0 pm to 7-0 pm	6" NEWTON	1	Z.3
Trench C.14.a.00.75. to FLASH COT	9-0 am to 10-30 am	6" NEWTON	1	Z.1
Inner belt C.7.d.72.60. to C.7.d.80.40.	11-0 am to 12-30 pm	6" NEWTON	1	Z.2
Trench C.7.d.20.70. to C.7.d.40.70.	5-0 am to 7-0 am	2"	4	
Trench and invisible wire C.7.c.30.90. to C.7.c.40.90.	8-0 am to 11-0 am	2"	3	
Wire and trench C.7.c.70.80. to C.7.d.00.80.	6-0 am to 12-30 pm	2"	3	
Trench C.14.a.00.75. to FLASH COT	5-0 am to 9-0 am	2"	3	
Wire C.14.a.35.40. to C.14.a.40.22.	11-0 am to 12-30 pm	2"	1	
Trench C.7.d.95.20. to C.13.b.98.98.	5-0 am to 12-30 pm	2"	7.	

17-7-17.

                                                   Captain R.F.A.
                                                  D.T.M.O. 38th Division.

T.M. 1/3.

Right Divisional Artillery Trench Mortars.
BOMBARDMENT SCHEME FOR 17-7-17.

HEAVY T.M. GROUP.

Target	Time.	No. of. Guns.	
Trench Junction C.7.a.70.40.	5-0 am to 7-30 am	1 - 9.45" T.M.	H.4.
Group of trenches around Junction of CADDIE SUPPORT and CADDIE TRENCH and KIEL COT.	9-0 am to 11-30 am	1 - 9.45" T.M.	H.3.
THE MOUND.	2-0 pm to 5-0 pm	1 - 9.45" T.M.	H.1.
Wire around THE MOUND.	6-0 am to 8-0 am	1 - 6" NEWTON T.M.	Z.3.
Inner belt of wire FLASH COT to C.14.a.30.49.	9-0 am to 11-0 am	1 - 6" Newton T.M.	Z.1.
Wire C.7.d.10.70. to KIEL COT.	11-30 am to 12-30 pm	1 - 6" Newton T.M.	Z.2.

LEFT MEDIUM T.M. GROUP.

Target	Time	No. of Guns
Wire round THE MOUND	5-0 am to 8-0 am	2 - 2" T.Ms.
Wire C.2.d.75.75. to C.7.c.95.75.	9-0 am to 12-30 pm	3 - 2" T.Ms.
Wire and trench C.7.d.40.65. to KIEL COT	10-0 am to 12-30 pm	4 - 2" T.Ms.

RIGHT MEDIUM T.M. GROUP.

Target	Time	No. of Guns
Wire inner belt C.7.d.75.55. to C.7.d.80.33.	5-0 am to 12-0 noon	4 - 2" T.Ms.
Wire inner belt C.7.d.95.05 to C.13.b.80.90.	9-0 am to 11-0 am (Intense searching fire)	4 - 2" T.Ms.
Wire inner belt FLASH COT to C.14.a.30.49.	9-0 am to 11-30 am	4 - 2" T.Ms.

14-7-17.

Captain R.F.A.
D.T.M.O. 36th Division.

Scheme for TM Bombardment
16-1-17

__Main M[?]__

C & C 15.85	9.00 a.t	
C y d 20.40	11.00 a.m	1 TM

Junction of Commie Support	11.30 a.t	1 minute
& Rifle Trench	11.31	

The Mound	4.0 a.t	1 min
	4.4 p.m	

Third wire N. of	11.30 a.t	1.6"
Forsan Cut	12.36 p.m	quarter TM

Wire C 12.15.85	5.4 pm t	1.6"
F C y d 20.45	7.4 pm	minute TM

__Right MTM (Group)__
Commence after Prelude

C 14 a 10.60 t	6.0 am	Four
C 14 a 25.75	8.0 am	2 TMs
10 m Rifle Cort	8.0 am t	Four
C y d 80.40	10.0 am	2 TMs
Wire C 14 a 21.50 t	10.30 am t	Four
C 14 a 35.30	12.30 pm	2 TMs

[illegible handwritten notes on graph paper]

38th DIVISIONAL TRENCH MORTAR BATTERIES.

OPERATION ORDER No. 1.

Reference Sheet 28 N.W.

1. V/61/T.M.B. will relieve V/20/T.M.B. in the line on the 15th inst., and will take over positions as follows :-

    L.1. -C.13.c.10.60.

    L.2. C.13.a.35.18.

    L.3. -C.13.a.30.70.

2. Relief to be completed by 2-0 pm. On completxion of relief V/61/T.M.B. will come under orders of O.C. Heavy T.M. Group. Pending completion of Battery Emplacements, personnel will be accomodated in COPSE B.23.d.70.60.

3. On completion of relief V/20/T.M.B. will remain in the line under O.C. Heavy T.M. Group in order to assist supply of ammunition and work in that Group.

4. All secret instructions and trench maps other than sheet 28 N.W 2 will be handed over on relief.

5. Please ACKNOWLEDGE.

O J Jones

Captain R.F.A.
D.T.M.O. 38th Division.

14-7-17.

Copies to :- O.C. Heavy T.M. Group (2)
D.T.M.O. 61st Division (2)
D.T.M.O. 20th Division
38th Div. Arty.
Diary.

T.M. 862.

BOMBARDMENT SCHEME.
HEAVY T.M. GROUP,
RIGHT DIVISION.

Heavy T.M. Batteries

No. of Guns.   6 Old pattern 9.45" T.M.
                                    1 New pattern 9.45" T.M.

Positions V/38/T.M.B.
- H.1. C.13.a.15.70.
- H.2. C.13.a.05.65.
- H.3. C.13.a.02.95.
- H.4. B.18.d.95.15.

V/30/T.M.B.
- L.1. C.13.a.10.60.
- L.2. C.13.a.35.15.
- L.4. C.13.a.70.70.

Targets.
1. The MOUND.
2. Salient at C.7.c.55.75.
3. Group of Trenches C.7.c.95.75. to C.7.d.25.70.
4. Trench Junction C.7.c.70.40.
5. CACTUS JUNCTION.
6. Group of trenches around junction of CADDIE SUPPORT and CADDIE TRENCH, KIEL COT, Sap at C.7.d.40.65.
7. CAESARS NOSE. Area – C.8.c.10.05. – C.7.d. 95.10. – C.13.b.90.90. – C.14.a.10.70. – C.14.a.25.60.

Time table.
- 15th.   Targets No. 3 and No. 6.
- 16th.   Targets No. 1, No. 2, and No. 7.
- 17th.   Targets No. 1, No. 4, and No. 7. Registration by aeroplane of CAESAR SUPPORT.
- 18th.   Targets No. 5, No. 6, and No. 7.
- 19th.   Targets No. 1, No. 3, and No. 7.

NOTE. Long range Heavy T.M. at position L.1. will be used experimentally towards end of bombardment to engage PILCKEM.

6" Newton Battery.

No. of Guns   3.

Positions 3/38/T.M.B.
- N.1. C.13.a.45.30.
- N.2. C.13.a.50.40.
- N.3. C.13.a.05.80.

Targets. Wire.
1. C.7.c.15.85. to C.7.c.30.90.
2. C.7.c.85.75. to C.7.c.95.75.
3. Inner belt C.7.d.40.65. to C.7.d.30.20. paying special attention to masses of wire at KIEL COT.
4. C.13.b.90.90. to C.14.a.00.70.
5. Thick wire about C.14.a.05.65.

13-7-17

(Trenches).

T.M. 1/10.

RIGHT ARTILLERY TRENCH MORTARS

BOMBARDMENT PROGRAMME 21-7-17.

Target.	Time.	Calibre.	No. of guns.
Concrete dugout C.7.c.53.88. C.7.c.95.75.	8-0 am to 11-0 am	9.45"	3.
Concrete dugouts C.8.c.1.3. C.14.a.10.95. C.14.a.4.7. C.7.d.8.4. THE PIMPLE	8-0 am to 12-30 pm	9.45"	2
CABIN SUPPORT C.7.a.36.40. to C.7.a.50.20.	8-0 am to 11-0 am	9.45"	1
Hidden wire C.7.c.32.90. to C.7.c.52.75.	8-0 am to 11-0 am	6" NEWTON	1
Trench C.7.d.95.10. to C.13.b.8.8.	11-0 am to 12-30 pm	6" NEWTON	1
Bunches of wire still remaining C.14.a.31.41. to C.14.a.13.60.	8-0 am to 12-30 pm	2"	4
Wire C.8.c.05.05. to C.14.a.20.75.	8-0 am to 12-30 pm	2"	4
Wire visible from front line about C.7.d.80.80.	8-0 am to 12-30 pm	2"	4
Trench and wire C.7.c.32.90. to C.7.c.58.75.	8-0 am to 11-0 am	2"	4
Trench C.7.c.95.75. to C.7.d.05.65.	8-0 am to 12-30 pm	2"	4.

20-7-17.

Captain R.F.A.
D.T.M.O. 38th Division.

T.M. 1/13.

HEAVY ARTILLERY TRENCH MORTAR BATTERIES.

BOMBARDMENT PROGRAMME 22-7-17.

Target	Time	Calibre.	No. of Guns.
Concrete dugouts C.8.c.1.5. C.14.a.10.95. C.14.a.4.7. C.7.d.8.4. TIN PEOPLE.	9-30 am to 12-30 pm	9.45"	2
Front line C.7.d.20.70. to C.7.d.40.65.	9-30 am to 12-30 pm	9.45"	1
Front Line C.7.c.90.80. to C.7.d.05.70.	9-30 am to 12-30 pm	9.45"	2
FARM 14 Area	2-0 pm to 5-0 pm	9.45"	2
Trench and wire C.7.c.32.90. to C.7.c.52.70.	5-0 pm to 7-0 pm	6" NEWTON	1
Trench and wire C.7.c.32.90. to C.7.c.58.76.	11-0 am to 2-0 pm	2"	3
Trench C.7.c.58.78. to C.7.c.85.78.	6-0 am to 11-0 am	2"	3
Bunch of wire C.7.d.15.70.	8-0 am to 11-0 am	8-9 am in 2" 2Xk-3 am	3
Wire C.7.d.43.55. to C.7.d.76.50.	6-0 am to 10-30 am	2"	3
Trench and bunches of wire Point of CAESARS NOSE to FLASH COT	11-0 am to 12-30 pm	2"	4
Remaining bunches of wire C.14.a.31.41. to C.14.a.17.17.	6-0 am to 10-30 am	2"	3

21-7-17.

Captain R.F.A.
D.T.M.O. 38th Division.

T.M. 1/14.

RIGHT ARTILLERY TRENCH MORTAR BATTERIES.
BOMBARDMENT PROGRAMME 23-7-17.

Target.	Time.	Calibre.	No. of guns.
THE MOUND.	6-0 am to 8-0 am	9.45"	1
Dugouts around CAESARS NOSE	9-0 am to 12-30 pm	9.45"	2
Trench C.7.d.40.65. to C.7.d.55.60.	9-30 am to 12-30 pm	9.45"	2
Trench C.7.c.85.80. to C.7.d.00.75.	9-30 am to 12-30 pm	9.45"	2
Remaining wire at the MOUND	11-0 am to 2-0 pm	2"	3
Remaining wire at C.7.c.5.7. to C.7.c.6.7.	6-0 am to 8-0 am	2"	3
Remaining wire C.7.d.2.7. to C.7.d.3.7.	9-0 am to 11-0 am	2"	3
Wire C.7.d.45.55. to C.7.d.75.50.	10-0 am to 12-30 pm	2"	3
Trench and wire CAESAR SUPPORT C.8.c.10.25. to C.14.a.10.95.	10-0 am to 12-30 pm	2"	4
Trench and bunches of wire C.14.a.30.40. to C.14.a.45.15.	10-0 am to 12-30 pm	2"	1

O J Jones

Captain R.F.A.
D.T.M.O. 38th Division.

22-7-17.

T.M. 1/15.

TRENCH MORTARS. RIGHT ARTILLERY BOMBARDMENT PROGRAMME. 24-7-17.

Target.	Time.	Calibre.	No. of guns.
CAESAR RESERVE around MAUSER COT		9.45"	1
CAESAR RESERVE around C.8.c.15.25.		9.45"	1
CACTUS POINT to C.7.b.75.30.		9.45"	2
THE MOUND	5-0 pm to 7-0 pm	9.45"	1
THE MOUND	10-0 am to 11-0 am.	6" NEWTON	1 (Registration)
Wire C.7.c.10.95. to C.7.c.2.8.	8-0 am to 11-0 am	2"	3
Invisible wire C.7.c.32.90.to C.7.c.58.78.	6-0 pm to 7-0 pm	2"	3
Bunch of wire C.7.d.30.60.	10-0 am to 12-30 pm	2"	2
CAIDIE SUPPORT. Trench and wire C.7.d.85.60. to C.8.c.05.80.	7-0 am to 12-30 pm	2"	3
CAESAR SUPPORT C.14.a.25.80. to C.14.a.45.65.	9-0 am to 12-30 pm	2"	4
Front Line C.14.a.30.40. to C.14.a.45.20.	6-0 am to 12-30 pm	2"	4

23-7-17.

Captain R.F.A.
D.T.M.O. 36th Division.

T.M. 1/17.

RIGHT ARTILLERY TRENCH MORTAR BATTERIES.

BOMBARDMENT PROGRAMME 25-7-17.

Target.	Time.	Calibre.	No. of Guns.
CAESAR RESERVE from MAUSER COT to C.8.c.15.25.	12-0 noon to 3-0 pm	9.45"	2
Junction of CACTUS RESERVE and CADDIE RESERVE C.7.d.05.95.	6-0 am to 9-0 am	9.45"	1
CABLE SUPPORT C.7.a.34.42. to C.7.a.48.22.	2-0 pm to 5-0 pm	9.45"	1
New work in CACTUS TRENCH C.7.c.65.77. to C.7.d.00.76.	12-0 am to 12-30 pm	9.45"	1
CACTUS AVENUE C.7.b.15.68. to C.1.d.10.10.	12-0 noon to 3-0 pm	6" NEWTON	3
CABLE SUPPORT C.7.a.55.22. to C.7.a.45.39.	6-0 am to 9-0 am	2"	3
CACTUS TRENCH C.7.c.95.77. to C.7.d.05.76.	11;0 am to 12-30 pm	2"	3
CADDIE SUPPORT C.7.d.80.75. to junction with front line.	between 11-30 am to 12-30 pm	2"	3
New work C.7.d.75.55. to C.7.d.90.23.	12-0 am to 12-30 pm	2"	3
CAESAR RESERVE Near junction with CAESARS AVENUE C.14.a.60.80.	12-0 noon to 3-0 pm	2"	
Front Line C.14.a.55.20. to C.14.a.70.05.	11-0 am to 12-30 pm	2"	

Captain R.T.A.
D.T.M.O. 20th Division.

24-7-17.

T.M. 2/24.

RIGHT ARTILLERY TRENCH MORTAR BATTERIES.
BOMBARDMENT PROGRAMME 26-7-17.

Target.	Time.	Calibre.	No. of guns.
Junction of GUDRUN AVENUE and GUDRUN TRENCH.	3-0 pm to 6-0 pm	9.45"	1
Hostile front line C.14.a.35.35. to C.14.a.50.15.	3-0 pm to 6-0 pm	2"	4

25-7-17.

Captain R.F.A.
D.T.M.O. 38th Division.

T.M. 1/21.

RIGHT ARTILLERY TRENCH MORTAR BATTERIES.

BOMBARDMENT PROGRAMME 27-7-17.

Target	Time.	Calibre	No. of guns
Belt of wire in front of THE MOUND.	8-0 am to 10-0 am	2"	3
Registration of THE MOUND	10-0 am to 11-0 am	2"	9

O J Jones
Captain R.F.A.
D.T.M.O. 38th Division.

26-7-17.

38th DIVISIONAL TRENCH MORTAR BATTERIES.

OPERATION ORDER No. 5.

1. On the night of the 30th inst. T.Ms. will engage targets as follows :-

   V/20/T.M.B.   9-0 am to 2-0 pm. CACTUS RESERVE and CADDIE
                                   RESERVE. Bursts of fire.

   Z/38/T.M.B.   9-0 am to 12 noon CAESAR RESERVE.
                 1-0 pm to 4-0 pm CADDIE POINT.

   X/38/T.M.B.   9-0 am to 1-0 pm CAESAR RESERVE near HAUSER COT.
                                   Bursts of fire.

2. On conclusion of the above programme, all T.M. personnel East of the CANAL BANK will withdraw to WEST CANAL BANK, dumping at Battery dumps all guns and gunstores that they cannot carry back with them. 2" T.M. beds in position will not be pulled up. All T.M. personnel must be across the CANAL by 5-0 pm. Batteries will then return to Billets, with the exception of

   1. Z/38/T.M.B. who will remain in action.

   2. 2/Lieut H. Musker R.G.A. and 2 men of X/38/T.M.B. who will guard 38th Div. T.M. Stores.

   3. One Officer and two O.R. of 20th Div. who will guard 20th Div. T.M. stores.

   4. One Officer and two men of V/20/T.M.B. who will guard Heavy T.M. Stores.

3. Units moving out of the line must be clear of the CANAL BANK by 7-0 pm. No T.M. Personnel will circulate on the CANAL BANK between the hours of 9-0 pm and 12-0 midnight.

4. D.T.M.O. will remain on CANAL BANK at B.24.b.1.3. until 12 noon on the 31st inst. when he will move to T.M. Billets A.17.a.9.1.

29-7-17.

Captain R.F.A.
D.T.M.O. 38th Division.

Bombardment Reports

15 - 31 July 1917

III

GAS TARGETS   Pros

Rifle Gren. Op. A Bombardment 15/7
                                    TARGET
Right M.M. Group   176 rounds   Hun C.T. e. 80. 84
                                    " C.T. a. 00. 76

Results
    Firing was accurate & effective. Target
    except for a small patch 50 yards long
    at C.T. e. 80. 7. Blown from
    HAPPY TRENCH.

Left M.M. Group   81 rounds   Hun Od. trench
                                C.T. u. 55. a. T C.T. u.
                                a. 65.
Results
    Shooting was ineffective owing to loss
    of known our observers. F.O. officer
    only be quite fair in daylight. Observed
    from Post 36.

Heavy M Group   10 rounds   CACTUS TRENCH
Results
    4 direct hits on trench in the
    neighbourhood. Observed from Post 36.

                                        O.J. Forster
15/7/17   Capt. R.F.A.
                                        OTMC SMAIS

BOMBARDMENT REPORT (Not to include Counter Battery Work)

From Noon 16/17-7-17......1917.

Calibres.	No. of Rounds.	Objective.	Method of Observation.	Remarks. (Gaps in wire, damage to trenches etc)
9.45" T.M.	26	THE MOUND.	From POST 36	Considerable damage was done to this target as several direct hits were obtained mainly about 6.7.a.20.95.
9.45" T.M.	7	CACTUS JUNCTION and Junction of trench junction G.7.a.4.20	From POST 36	1 Hit on CACTUS JUNCTION and 1 hit 10 yards from trench junction.
9.45" T.M.	25	Junction of CACTUS TRENCH BEFORE with CACTUS TRENCH, and NORTH 19.	From POST 36	18 effective rounds were observed.
6" NEWTON	82	Wire round THE MOUND.	From POST 35	Direct observation of the wire was very difficult but judging from the amount of wire and stakes thrown up during the shooting was very effective. Damage caused to the western face of the Mound.
6" NEWTON.	60	Wire round THE MOUND.	From POST 34.	Considerable damage to trench and wire.
6" NEWTON	34	Wire G.7.d.10.70. to KILL COT.		

Capt R.F.A.
A.T.M.O. 36 Divn

BOMBARDMENT REPORT (Not to include Counter Battery Work)

From Noon 16/17-7-17 to Noon ....1917.

Calibres.	No. of Rounds.	Objective.	Method of Observation.	Remarks. (Gaps in wire, damage to trenches etc)
2" T.M.	40	Wire from C.7.c.20.90. to C.7.c.54.95.	From line	Details not received.
2" T.M.	100	Wire as per ABOVE	POST 35	Large amount of wire and stakes displaced. Exact damage not visible.
2" T.M.	142	Wire C.7.c.75.75. to C.7.c.95.75	POST 35	80 yards of wire cleared and other gaps made about C.7.c.80.65. 70% of the rounds fired were effective.
2" T.M.	180	Wire and trench C.7.d.40.45. to WIRE CUT.	POST 16	Details of results not received. But about 65 rounds were effective.
2" T.M.	300	Wire C.7.d.75.5. to C.7.d.90.35.	Target almost invisible	This fire was directed against an area. This area was well swept.
2" T.M.	274	Wire FLASH COT to C.14.c.30.40	From Front Line	Wire well cleared around FLASH COT but there are still some small bunches around C.14.c.35.35.
2" T.M.	128	Wire C.7.d.75.55. to C.7.d.80.35.	POST 35	No details received as to results.
	1164			

BOMBARDMENT REPORT (Not to include Counter Battery Work)

From Noon to Noon ......17/18 July......1917.

Calibres.	No. of Rounds.	Objective.	Method of Observation.	Remarks. (Gaps in wire, damage to trenches etc)
9.45"	50	THE MOUND	POST 36	Accurate observation extremely difficult owing to lack of cable to connect up with O.P. About 25 hits obtained on trenches in and about the MOUND.
9.45"	20	SUNKEN SUPPORTS around C.14.a.35.75.	CONTOUR 19	Light very bad. 10 rounds appeared to fall in or near the trench.
6" NEWTON	13	Trench C.14.a.00.75. to FLASH ORN.	CONTOUR 19.	Effect on target not visible.
6" NEWTON	24	Wire C.7.d.92.82. to C.7.d.90.20.	POST 36.	Several large gaps made in wire on this target.
2"	120	Trench C.7.d.20.70. to C.7.d.90.70.	POST 36	80% of the rounds fired were effective and a large amount of timber was thrown up. This trench appears to be very much knocked about.

BOMBARDMENT REPORT (Not to include Counter Battery Work)

From Noon 17/18 July 1917.

Calibres.	No. of Rounds.	Objective.	Method of Observation.	Remarks. (Gaps in wire, damage to trenches etc)
6"	120	Trench and wire C.7.c.30.90. to C.7.c.40.90.	POST 33	Effect Invisible but large amounts of material and wire was thrown up.
6"	270	Wire and trench C.7.c.70.80. to C.7.d.00.80.	POST 33	Effect Excellent. The wire was considerably thinned and much timber displaced. Clear gap made in wire about C.7.d.00.80.
6"	218	Trench C.14.a.00.75. to FLASH GUN	O.P. C.14.c.4.9.	Known completely destroyed. 75% direct hits.
6"	95	Wire C.14.a.33.40. to C.14.a.40.22.	O.P. C.14.c.4.9.	Wire badly damaged but some small bunches still remain.
6"	450	Trench C.7.d.95.20. to C.13.b.90.95.	O.P. C.14.c.4.9.	This target was destroyed.
	1252			

Orange

Captain R.F.A.
D.L.M.O. 38th Division.

From Noon ...18/19.7..... 1917.

BOMBARDMENT REPORT (Not to include Counter Battery Work)

Calibres.	No. of Rounds.	Objective.	Method of Observation.	Remarks. (Gaps in wire, damage to trenches etc)
9.45"	12	CACTUS JUNCTION area	POST 36	4 hits on trench about C.7.b.9.5. Gun out of action.
9.45"	10	CACTUS JUNCTION area	Unobserved	All lines out by last night's bombardment
9.45"	15	C.7.a.80.20. to CACTUS JUNCTION	Unobserved	All lines out by last night's bombardment.
9.45"	40	Area around KIEL COF	POST 38	These trenches now appear to be obliterated as far as ground observation goes. One concrete was destroyed.
9.45"	50	The MOUND	POST 39	35th on MOUND. Nothing seen in trenches.
9.45"	35	Area round C.4.c.10.05.	POST 19	xxxxxxxxxxxxxxxxxxxx xxxxxxxxxxxxxxxxx to bad light. Reported abnormal short in our lines.

BOMBARDMENT REPORT (Not to include Counter Battery Work)

From Noon ....1917.

Calibres.	No. of Rounds.	Objective.	Method of Observation.	Remarks. (Gaps in wire, damage to trenches etc)
6" NEWTON	140	Wire about H19 NORTH	POST 29	First really effective shoot on to this wire. This wire is thick and has been considerably thinned.
6" NEWTON	80	Trench C.7.d.75.55.	POST 36	Considerable damage has been done to this trench.
6" NEWTON	90	TRENCH.13.b.65.62. to 13.b.05.75.	HAIG TRENCH	Considerable damage to Front line + Chyauts – in progress
2"	97 & 100	Wire C.7.d.65.50. to C.7.d.05.65.	POST 33	3/4 effective rounds until 2 detachments were put out of action by Minenwerfer 10 feet above the muzzle. Another Battery then took up this target and fired 150 rounds.
2"	112	Trench C.7.d.10.70. to C.7.d.55.60.		Shoot still in progress.
2"	140	Wire at H19 NORTH		Shoot still in progress.
2"	220	Trench C.14.a.30.55. to C.14.a.30.40.	HAIG TRENCH	Trench completely destroyed on whole area of this target.

From Noon to Noon 18/19 July 1917.

BOMBARDMENT REPORT (Not to include Counter Battery Work)

Calibres.	No. of Rounds.	Objective.	Method of Observation.	Remarks. (Gaps in wire, damage to trenches etc
2"	90	Trench C.13.b.90.90. to C.7.d.93.05.		Timber and material thrown about, as usual. Lack of ammunition prevented further shooting.
2"	163	Trench C.7.d.85.35. to C.7.d.65.20.		Unobserved owing to bad light.

Captain R.F.A.
D.T.M.O. 46th Division.

BOMBARDMENT REPORT (Not to include Counter Battery Work)

From Noon 19/20 July, 1917.

Calibres.	No. of Rounds.	Objective.	Method of Observation.	Remarks. (Gaps in wire, damage to trenches etc)
2"	50	C.7.c.45.90. to C.7.c.72.80. Trench		Special attention paid to concrete dugout at C.7.c.60.80. with no visible effect.
2"	120	Trench C.7.d.10.65. to C.7.d.40.65.		40% effective rounds.
2"	120	C.7.d.80.40. to C.7.d.90.20. Trench.		Considerable damage in neighbourhood of dugout C.7.d.80.40.
2"	105	Dugouts around CAESAR'S NOSE		Several hits on dugouts at C.13.b.80.85. C.14.a.10.75., with no visible effect.
2"	68	Trench and wire FLASH COT to C.14.a.30.40.		Wire completely destroyed for about 30 yards from C.14.a.05.60. to C.14.a.35.40. Two direct hits on dugout at C.14.a.10.65., one end blown away.

Captain R.F.A.
D.T.M.O. 38th Division

BOMBARDMENT REPORT (Not to include Counter Battery Work)

From Noon to Noon 19/20 July............1917.

Calibres.	No. of Rounds.	Objective.	Method of Observation.	Remarks. ((Gaps in wire, damage to trenches etc))
9.45"	27	Concrete dugouts near CACTUS JUNCTION.		Considerable damage to trench. One direct hit on a concrete dugout.
9.45"	40	JUNCTION of CABLE and CACTUS Trenches C.7.c.55.75.		Several direct hits on front line. Two abnormal shorts.
9.45"	40	Trench C.7.d.45.65. to C.7.d.65.72.		Two concrete dugouts destroyed and trench badly damaged.
9.45"	25	CAESAR SUPPORT C.8.c.10.35. to C.8.c.25.80.		No exact details received of damage done.
6" NEWTON	72	Wire at the MOUND (5-0 pm to 7-0 pm 19th)		Wire considerably damaged but a certain amount still remains to be cut.
6" NEWTON	52	Trench and wire C.14.a.30.40. to C.14.a.45.15.		Front line breached in several places and a good deal of timber thrown up.
6" NEWTON	99	Trench and wire C.7.d.65.50. to C.7.d.80.40.		Front line breached in several places and a good deal of timber thrown up.

From Noon to Noon .... 20/21 July, 1917.

BOMBARDMENT REPORT (Not to include Counter Battery Work)

Calibres.	No. of Rounds.	Objective.	Method of Observation.	Remarks. (Gaps in wire, damage to trenches etc)
9.45"	25	Dugouts C.7.c.53.88.		Only slight damage as gun was firing at minimum range.
9.45"	24	Dugout C.7.a.95.75.		Heavy timber thrown up three times and concrete structure seems to be broken up.
9.45"	30	Dugouts near CACTUS JUNCTION		One concrete dugout badly damaged
9.45"	65	Dugouts in CAESAR SUPPORT C.8.c. and C.14.a.		No direct hits were obtained but considerable damage was done to the whole trench line.
9.45"	27	Dugout C.7.c.55.88.		Dugout is inside minimum range of all guns but 7 hits were obtained on trench near it.
9.45"	33	C.7.b.35.45.		Nine direct hits on trench and one on trolley line. One German ran away across country at end of shoot. Communication cut.
9.45"	7	Dugout at C.7.c.85.75.		Two hits obtained on track.

From Noon to Noon .... 1917.
20/21 July.

BOMBARDMENT REPORT (Not to include Counter Battery Work)

Calibres.	No. of Rounds.	Objective.	Method of Observation.	Remarks. (Gaps in wire, damage to trenches etc)
6" NEWTON	104	Trench and wire C.7.c.30.75. to C.7.c.30.90.		Much wire and material was thrown into the air.
6" NEWTON	97	Trench C.7.d.95.10. to C.13.b.80.85.		Excellent results. Material of all sorts including two men being thrown into the air.
STOKES 2"	95	Trench and wire C.7.c.32.30. to C.7.c.52.75.		Target difficult to observe but much wire and material was displaced.
2"	231	Trench and wire C.7.c.32.90. to C.7.c.56.78.		Over 60% of the rounds fired seemed to be effective, and a considerable amount of wire was thrown into the air. Structure at C.7.c.30.45. destroyed.
2"	80	Trench C.7.c.95.75. to C.7.d.05.65.		About 30 hits on trench. Further firing impossible owing to lack of ammunition.

251 / 657

BOMBARDMENT REPORT (Not to include Counter Battery Work)

From Noon ....1917.
to Noon.
20/21 July.

Calibres.	No. of Rounds.	Objective.	Method of Observation.	Remarks. (Gaps in wire, damage to trenches etc)
2"	15	Wire C.14.a.31.41. to C.14.a.25.60.	ICEMB TRENCH C.14.a.20.15.	Bunch of wire visible against skyline completely cleared. Remaining bunches could not be dealt with owing to lack of ammunition.
2"	83	Wire CAESAR SUPPORT C.8.c.05.05 to C.14.a.30.75.		Target invisible.
2"	153 / 251	Wire C.7.d.45.55. to C.7.d.75.50.	POST 51.	Wire was thick in places and has been cleared KIEL COT and sap at C.7.d.40.55. There is still a good deal of wire round the latter place, and one bunch in front of KIEL COT. Both these patches were thinned today. Rounds were also fired into the small re-entrant south of KIEL COT but there does not appear to be any wire there, though a few broken stakes are visible in places.

Captain R.F.A.
D.T.M.O. 38th Division.

BOMBARDMENT REPORT (Not to include counter battery work)

From noon to noon 21/22-7-17.

Calibres.	No. of rounds.	Objective.	Method of observation.	Remarks. (Gaps in wire damage to trenches etc
9.45"	32	C.7.c.95.80. to C.7.c.75.80.		Considerable damage done to whole trench line. Three rounds fell within 10 yards of concrete dugout but failed to destroy it.
9.45"	18	C.7.c.60.75. to C.7.c.75.80.		Effective shooting was obtained on to this portion of trench.
9.45"	10	C.7.d.30.70. to C.7.d.40.60.		Gun very erratic, and eventually had to cease fire.
9.45"	40	Dugouts from C.14.a.20.80. to C.8.c.10.08.		Considerable damage to CAESAR SUPPORT between these points. 1 direct hit on THE PIMPLE.
2"	99	Trench and wire C.7.c.32.90. to C.7.c.85.78.		Good shooting once more obtained on to this target; material and wire thrown up from the portion in dead ground.
2"	60	Bunch of wire C.7.d.15.70.		Most of the rounds fired were effective but there are still one or two small clumps of wire remaining. One T.M. put out of action by a direct hit be hostile Artillery.
2"	100	Trench C.7.c.32.90 to C.7.c.58.78.		Shoot still in progress.
2"	51 (All available)	Wire at point of CAESARS NOSE and in front of CAESAR SUPPORT C.14.a.10.95 to C.14.a.30.70.		Not sufficient ammunition available for any definite results.
2"	150	Wire C.14.a.47.17. to C.14.a.31.41.		All visible wire has now been cleared from this front with the exception of one small bunch. One gun destroyed by hostile shell fire. One gun destroyed by premature.

Captain R.F.A.
D.T.M O. 38th Division.

Calibres.	No. of rounds.	Objective.	Method of observation.	Remarks.
2"	45	Wire C.7.d.45.45. to C.7.d.75.50.		Insufficient ammunition for an effective shoot,

22-7-17.

Captain R.F.A.
D.T.M.O. 38th Division.

BOMBARDMENT REPORT.

(Not to include counter battery work)

From noon to noon 22/23-7-17.

Calibres.	No. of rounds.	Objective.	Observed from.	Remarks.
9.45"	35	Wire in front of CABLE TRENCH.		Wire is not visible here, but stakes and trench material were frequently thrown up
9.45"	22	'NEST' about C.7.d.15.85.		This is not visible, but material was seen on 3 occasions so presumably something was hit.
9.45"	20	Trench from C.7.c.95.75. to C.7.c.80.80.		Trench was badly knocked about along whole target.
9.45"	11	C.7.d.50.60.		Only 11 rounds were fired on to this target, 10 of them being very effective. Mortar was then knocked out of action by hostile shell-fire.
9.45"	15	C.14.a.25.85. to C.8.c.10.00.		Material was thrown up several times, & trench appears to be obliterated.
9.45"	40	C.8.c.10.00. to C.8.c.15.25.		Good results along whole of target.
2"	50	Wire C.7.c.5.7. to C.7.c.6.7.		Good results, but this bunch of wire was not completely destroyed.
2"	75	wire C.7.d.2.7. to C.7.d.3.7.		Hostile shell fire having destroyed 3 guns of this battery this shoot was not very effective.
2"	250	Wire C.7.c.5.7. to C.7.c.6.7.		Shoot still in progress.
2"	65	C.14.a.30.40. to C.14.a.45.15.	POST 23a	The wire on this target is now no obstacle. Several hits were obtained on trench.
2"	100	Wire C.8.c.10.25 to C.14.a.10.95.	POST 25	Target invisible but judging from the amount of wire thrown into the air, the results were good.

Captain R.F.A.
D.T.M.O. 38th Division.

2"	65	Wire C.7.d.45.55.to C.7.d.75.50.	POST 51.	Southern portion of this target is now so ~~mhstash~~ damaged as to form no obstacle. It is possible that this wire is behind the hostile front line.

Captain R.F.A.
D.T.M.O. 38th Division.

RIGHT ARTILLERY TRENCH MORTAR BATTERIES.

BOMBARDMENT REPORT.

From noon to noon 23/24 July 1917.

Calibres.	No. of rounds.	Objective.	Remarks.
9.45"	20	CAESAR RESERVE near MAUSER COT	Observation very poor. It was found impossible to get further south than C.14.a.45.95.
9.45"	15	POST at C.7.d.18.88.	Material thrown up on three occasions.
9.45"	45	CACTUS POINT	Observation impossible, but much material was thrown up.
2"	113	Wire C.7.c.32.90. to C.7.c.58.78.	This wire now seems to be entirely cleared away.
2"	100	Wire C.7.d.30.40.	Shoot still in progress.
2"	77	CADDIE SUPPORT C.7.d.85.60. to C.8.c.05.30.	Target invisible, but a good deal of material was displaced.
2"	53	CAESAR SUPPORT C.14.a.25.80. to C.14.a.45.65.	Target invisible but duckboards and wire were thrown up by at least 40 of the rounds fired.
2"	150	Front Line C.14.a.30.40. to C.14.a.45.20.	Shoot seemed very effective judging from the amount of material displaced.

Captain R.F.A.
D.T.M.O. 38th Division.

RIGHT ARTILLERY TRENCH MORTAR BATTERIES.

BOMBARDMENT REPORT.

Noon to Noon 24/25 . 7 .17.

Calibres.	No. of rounds.	Objective.	Remarks.
9.45"	45	C.8.c.15.25.	Results not visible owing to poor light.
9.45"	23	C.7.d.98.85.	Target invisible, but results appeared to be good as timber was thrown up by six rounds.
2"	41	CABLE SUPPORT C.7.a.55.22. to C.7.a.45.20.	Visibility was poor but a fair number of effective rounds were observed.
2"	99	C.7.c.32.90. to C.7.c.58.78.	40 % Effective rounds.
2"	?	CANDLE SUPPORT C.7.d.60.75. to junction with front line.	Shoot still in progress.
2"	40	Trench C.14.a.35.20. to C.14.a.70.05.	Observation difficult owing to smoke. As far as can be ascertained considerable damage was done.

NOTE. Heavy T.M. shoot on CACTUS TRENCH was found to be impossible owing to communications being cut by hostile retaliation for this morning's barrage.

25-7-17.

2/Lt. R.F.A.
Captain R.F.A.
D.T.M.O. 38th Division.

RIGHT ARTILLERY TRENCH MORTAR BATTERIES.

BOMBARDMENT REPORT.

From noon to noon 25-26.7.17.

Calibre.	No. of rounds.	Objective.	Remarks.
9.45"	24	MAUSER COT	Target invisible and light very poor, but rounds all detonated well near the target.
9.45"	20	C.8.c.15.25.	-do-
6" NEWTON	32	B.12.d.95.80. to C.7.c.10.95.	Owing to lines being cut as fast as they were being mended, fire could not be opened till 6-30 pm, with observation by orderly from CANAL BANK. A quantity of material was thrown up.
2"	18	Trench B.12.d.97.90. to C.7.c.12.90.	10 hits on trench.
2"	40	Trench C.7.d.75.55. to C.7.d.90.25.	A good deal of timber thrown up about C.7.d.80.35. and neighbour-hood, also some loose wire and stakes from shorts. Some duds. Enemy retaliated heavily through-out with 15 cm how. Damage Nil.
2"	80	Trench C.14.a.60.80.	Three guns only were in action owing to one emplacement being obliterated by a 15 cm how. After about 12 rounds enemy retal-iated heavily with 15 cm H.E. Two more emplacements were blown in. Remaining gun continued firing with good effect, wood being thrown into the air. After half an hour another gun was dug out and commenced firing with good effect.

Captain R.F.A.
D.T.M.O. 38th Division.

RIGHT ARTILLERY TRENCH MORTAR BATTERIES.

BOMBARDMENT REPORT.

Noon to noon 26- 27.7.17.

Calibre.	No. of rounds.	Objective.	Remarks.
9.45"	25	C.8.c.80.40.	Unobserved.
2"	90	Trench C.14.a.35.35. to C.14.a.50.15.	Good results. Timber thrown up. Enemy retaliated heavily with 15 cm how. and 77 mm gun firing gas shells.
2"	4	Front Line. THE MOUND. C.7.c.25.98. to C.7.c.23.85. C.7.c.23.85. to C.7.c.15.95.	Registration. All communications cut and shoot could not proceed. Rounds fired were effective.
2"	45	Wire in hollow in front of MOUND.	This wire was cleared.
2"	124	The MOUND	Registration.

Captain R.F.A.
D.T.M.O. 38th Division.

SUPPLEMENTARY REPORT.

9.45"	5	MAUSER COT and surroundings.	Firing could not be continued as the pit was destroyed by shock of discharge of the 5th round.
6" NEWTON	106	C.14.a.55.85. to C.8.c.20.25.	This trench is not visible from either CONTOUR 19 or the O.P. at bridge 6.A. After a little adjustment from map range, a large quantity of wood and trench boards were thrown up. The trench was covered by a series of switches from MAUSER COT.

RIGHT ARTILLERY TRENCH MORTAR BATTERIES.

BOMBARDMENT REPORT.

Noon to noon 28 - 29-7-17.

Calibre	No. of rounds.	Target.	Remarks.
9.45"	30	CACTUS RESERVE	Bursts of fire.
9.45"	?	CACTUS and CADDIE Reserves.	Bursts of fire. Shoot still in progress.
6" NEWTON	?	CADDIE SUPPORT	Bursts of fire. Shoot still in progress.
2"	?	CAESAR SUPPORT CAESAR RESERVE.	Bursts of fire. Shoot still in progress.

29-7-17.

Captain R.F.A.
D.T.M.O. 38th Division.

RIGHT ARTILLERY TRENCH MORTAR BATTERIES.

BOMBARDMENT REPORT.

Noon to noon 29 - 30.7.17.

Calibre.	No. of. rounds.	Target.	Remarks.
9.45"	57	CACTUS RESERVE CADDIE RESERVE	Target invisible.
6" NEWTON	200	CADDIE POINT GALLWITZ FARM	It is difficult to observe these targets, but a series of switches and alterations in range were made to search the ground around these targets. Retaliation fairly heavy.
6" NEWTON	300	CADDIE POINT CAESAR RESERVE	-do-
2"	150	CAESAR SUPPORT CAESAR RESERVE Neighbourhood of KIEL COT	Ground between trenches was searched and an endeavour made to damage the enemy who were reported to be in shell holes in this vicinity. Enemy was seen to send up VERY lights.

O J Jones
Captain R.F.A.
D.T.M.O. 38th Division.

INTELLIGENCE SUMMARY RIGHT GROUP 38TH.D.A.
1.a.m. 30.6.17. to 11.a.m. 1.7.17.
----------ooOoo----------

ENEMY.
Throughout the day and night.
At 4.55.p.m. CANAL BANK, SKIPTON and HUDDERSFIELD TRENCHES were shelled by 77.mm.Guns and 10.5.cm.How Batteries. In reply to this, we concentrated all Batteries on JOLIE FARM and STRAY FARM, firing about 50 rounds rapidly, & enemy shelling ceased shortly afterwards.
CANAL BANK was again shelled by 10.5.cm.How Battery, 24 rounds.
Canal Bank and Communication trenches were shelled at intervals during the night and early morning.
Details of all hostile shelling and bearings have been reported direct to XIV Corps R.A. Counter Battery Staff Officer.
About 12 mid-night about 100 rounds were fired at TROIS TOURS CHATEAU. Several rounds falling in the Moat. Little damage.
At 7.a.m. (1st.July) 13.cm.Gun, bearing about 58° True from E.B.30., opened in single rounds slowly, firing Air bursts, evidently attempting to register 6" Howitzers in TROIS TOURS Drive. This continued until 9.30.a.m., when rapid rate of ground bursts was opened. Mostly short. About 30% were blind. This continued until 10.30.a.m. when the shelling ceased. About 500 rounds were fired. This gun was firing at a very long range.

OUR ARTILLERY.
Wirecutting with 106 Fuze.

1) With the object of testing this fuze at a short range, one Gun "B"/122 was moved forward to position near WAGON FARM at B.18.c.3.8. on the night 29th/30th., and fired on enemy wire in front of CACTUS TRENCH C 7.c.55.75.
The range to this point was 1600 yards. Difficulty was experienced in clearing the trees on the Canal Bank, and owing to this it was not possible to engage the wire further to the left as I had hoped, where the range would only have been about 1200 yards. At a range of 1600 yards however, the destructive effect of this ammunition on wire was even more marked than at longer ranges. Wire and stakes were removed wholesale, detonations being consistently good. No backward effect was noticed, but a certain amount of forward, in addition to large lateral effect, was evident.

2) "A"/122 fired 154 rounds at wire about C.14.a.15.85. Range 2900-3100 yards.
Large gap about 20 yards wide was cleared and a smaller gap to the right.
Only one round failed to detonate.

Other points shelled were:-
JOLIE FARM, which was bombarded by all Batteries.
CANDLE TRENCH, burst of harassing fire by 3 batteries during the night.
MACHINE GUN EMPLACEMENT C.14.a.15.90. - Several direct hits, but no damage.
CACTUS JUNCTION and CANCER TRENCH.
CANAL DRIVE C.1.c.85.20. - Movement seen at intervals.
HOUSE U.26.c.90.45. - Probable O.P. One direct hit with 4.5" How.
STRAY FARM & TRENCH Leading to. - Harassing fire during the night.

GENERAL. Owing to rain and mist observation was difficult.
The loophole at M.G. Emplacement C.14.a.15.90. is very noticeable. This is a concrete emplacement.
At 1.15.a.m. Corps on our right opened very heavy fire, the enemy firing a large number of Red rockets and replying.
18-Pounders with 106 Fuze have little or no effect on earthworks, enemy trenches or timber at ranges from 3000 yards upwards.
No enemy aeroplanes were up owing to bad weather.

GUNS OUT OF ACTION.
A)   One Gun "A"/122.   I.O.M. - Overhaul.
     One How "D"/122.   I.O.M. - Overhaul.
     One How "D"/121.   I.O.M.   Overhaul.
B) Nil.
C)   One How "D"/122 - Completely destroyed by premature but not yet replaced

GUNS IN ACTION.   "A"/122. - 5 Guns.   "D"/121. 5 Hows.
                    "B"/122. - 6 Guns.   "D"/122. 4 Hows.
                    "C"/122. - 6 Guns.
                    "C"/121. - 6 Guns.

N i l.

PERSONNEL & CASUALTIES.

One Other Rank slight wounded in "B"/142.
One N.C.O. c/R. wounded

Lieut.Colonel.R.F.A.
Commanding Right Group. 38th. D. A.

Urgent

Q/1019/22/2

D.T.M.O.

38th Division.

    Please detail 75 men to be attached to Brigades as under:-

  121st Brigade - - - 25 men.
  122nd Brigade - - - 25 men.
  76th Brigade - - - 25 men.

    Theyshould report to Right Group not later than 6 p.m. tomorrow 25th, and will remain with Brigades until further orders.

    Rations for consumption 26th must be taken.

              Captain R.A.
24th August 1917.   Staff Captain R.A. 38th Division.

Army Form C. 2118

WAR DIARY
or
INTELLIGENCE SUMMARY

(Erase heading not required.)

Vol 14

38 Divisional T.M. Batteries.

August 1917.

WAR DIARY
INTELLIGENCE SUMMARY

Army Form C. 2118

Place	Date	Hour	Summary of Events and Information	Remarks and references to Appendices
A17a9.1 Sheet 28 N.W.	8/1/17		Two Batteries "Z" under 2nd Lt G.F.HARRIS R.F.A. and "X" under 2nd Lt H.MUSKER R.F.A. remain in action at C19.a.03. Z Bty being equipped with 6" Newtons	
	2	9.0 pm	Motors, Stretcher Bearing parties relieved by 30 for the unit owing to incessant rain	
		6.0 pm	Further 30 men required for stretcher bearing under Lt GREY R.F.A.	
	3		All men up the line. Stretcher bearers except "X" & "Z" Batteries at C19.a.03	
	4	4 pm	Lt GREY relieves Lt HARRIS and all stretcher bearers are returned to Billets	
	4/5		Collection of stores, equipment and drying activities	
	6		All D.A.C. attached men returned X & Z Batteries come out & rest with the exception of 1 N.C.O. & gunner	
	7		All men & guns withdrawn from the line	
X29c7.1 Sheet 19	8		All men & guns with the exception of 2/Lt T.F.BRIGGS R.F.A. & 16 O.R. of Z 35 T.M.B. at X29C7.1 Sheet 19 move to SARAWAK Camp at X29C7.1 Sheet 19 2/Lt H.MUSKER	Appendix 1.
	9	3.0 pm	D.T.M.O + O.C "Z" Battery at R.H. regarding the mobility of 6" Newton. 2/Lt T.F.BRIGGS Salvaging 2" Bombs in Divisional area SARAWAK Camp	
	10		2.36 under 2/Lt T.F.BRIGGS move to SARAWAK Camp	
	11		2 Lt H. MUSKER R.F.A. wounded in action. 2/Lt R.H. DEWHIRST R.F.A replaces him in Salvaging T.M. Bombs	

WAR DIARY
or
INTELLIGENCE SUMMARY
(Erase heading not required.)

Army Form C. 2118

Instructions regarding War Diaries and Intelligence Summaries are contained in F.S. Regs., Part II. and the Staff Manual respectively. Title Pages will be prepared in manuscript.

Place	Date	Hour	Summary of Events and Information	Remarks and references to Appendices
X29 c 7. Sheet 19.	13/8/17		2 Lt R.H. DEWHIRST transferred from "Z" 38 & "V" 38. 2 Lt C.H. MOORE transferred from "X" & "Y" 38	
	14/8/17		Ostilis seasoned 1 gun stores by Isakhern	
	16		2 Lt C.H. MOORE granted leave to U.K. Capt L.W. FOX G.L. reports from leave	
			Lt B.V. CLARK RFA reports from Hospital. Batteries training.	
X30 d9 2 Sheet 19.	16		DTMO Capt O.J. JONES RFA granted leave to U.K. Capt L.W FOX G.L a/DTMO	
			3 TMB's move to STROUD camp X30 d 7.2	
	20		2 Lt W. EVANS RFA returns. 2 Lt DEWHIRST at salvaging bombs.	II
	20		Battalion training	
	24		Lt B.V. CLARK RFA granted leave to U.K.	
	24	10.0 am	2 Lt W. EVANS RFA (?) replaces Lt W.T.O BONNIWELL RFA (?) in B121, Bde RFA	
	25	4.0 pm	All available men make up parties ordered by OP 1079 2/2 70 ORs available	III
			3 Officers Lt W.T.O BONNIWELL RFA, 2Lt J.V. COLLINS RFA and 2Lt F.BRIGGS RFA report to OC D.A.C. at 6.0 pm	IV
	26		Count closed up 4 Prisoners tackled	
	27		2 Lt C.H. MOORE RFA on returns from leave	
	28	9.0 pm	Capt FOX summoned to RFA refuses moving 6" Newton to LANGEMARCK.	
	29		Z 38 move forward taking gun sled to CANAL BANK. Lt G.S. HARRIS in command	
			Gun taken forward at night. S.J. Church in LANGEMARCK	

WAR DIARY
or
INTELLIGENCE SUMMARY.
(Erase heading not required.)

Army Form C. 2118.

Place	Date	Hour	Summary of Events and Information	Remarks and references to Appendices
X30 d 9.2 Sheet 19.	30/8/17	3.15 PM	6" Newton T.M. registered on Cemetery V.23.b.20.9.1 No retaliation	
	31	4 pm	Party of 25 OR report at camp from 76th F.A. Bde. Capt O.f.f. gave D.T.M.O returns from leave. Appendices IV	

O.T. For. Whams
2/Capt RFA
38 D TMO

SECRET.   RIGHT ARTILLERY.
INSTRUCTIONS NO. 1.

August 7th, 1917.

1.   (a) The 20th and 38th Divisional Trench Mortars (less one 6" Newton and detachment) will proceed to rest and training tomorrow, 8th instant.

    (b) They will be billeted in SARAWAK CAMP, X.29.c.7.1. (sheet 19).

2.   All trench mortars, less one 6" Newton, will accompany the personnel.

3.   The D.T.M.O. 38th Division will arrange that one 6" Newton mortar with detachment, under a responsible officer, remains behind. A position should be reconnoitred for this mortar from which AU BON GITE and the houses on the AU BON GITE - LANGEMARCK Road can be engaged. The location of this position will be reported to this office as soon as possible.

    Further details as to ammunition supply, the building of the emplacement, and when the mortar will go into the line will be issued later.

4.   Details as to accomodation and transport will be arranged by the respective Staff Captains.

5.   ACKNOWLEDGE.

                                                   Major, R.A.
                                  Brigade Major, Right Artillery.

Copies issued to:-
XIVth Corps R.A.
20th Division.
38th Division.
38th D.A. (2).
D.T.M.O. 20th Divn.
D.T.M.O. 38th Divn.
Staff Captain.
Diary.

Appendix II

"A" Form
MESSAGES AND SIGNALS.

Army Form C. 2121 (in Pads of 100).

| TO | 38th D.A. | | |

| Sender's Number. | Day of Month. | In reply to Number. | |
| H. 510 | 18 | | A A A |

T.M. 38th Div to move to STROUD CAMP X.30.c.9.2. to-day AAA. Move to be completed by 6. p.m. AAA. ACKNOWLEDGE

Q 919/7

From R.A. 38th Div

Appendix III

WAR DIARY or INTELLIGENCE SUMMARY

38 D TM By Vol 15

Army Form C. 2118.

Place	Date	Hour	Summary of Events and Information	Remarks and references to Appendices
STROUD CAMP X/38 d g 2. Sheet 19	2.9.17		2/Lt W.S. HUNTER, Border Regt reports from the base and posted to 2/38 TMB. Lieut BONNIWELL posted to X/38 TMB. 2/Lt BRIGGS hands over to 2/Lt MOORE in the line. 2 O.R's wounded.	
	4.9.17		2/Lt E.J. MILLER WILLIAMS goes into the line. 2/Lt MOORE takes men salvage work. NCO and 14 men sent up for salvage work.	
	6.9.17		20th Division TM's take over 6" NEWTON + LAS TM's at STROUDCAMP X 30 d 12. Sheet 19	
	9.9.17		20th Division TM's take over all ammunition and equipment at LANGEMARK	
			at TM. DUMP. All men attached to Field Batteries report two guns 2/Lt E.J. MILLER-WILLIAMS goes on leave to UK.	
			Since 9th continued hostile aerial activity at night.	
	17.9.17		2/Lt J.V COLLINS granted leave to UK.	
	10.9.17		2/Lt F. BRIGGS granted leave to UK.	
	11.9.17		38th Divisional TM's move by motor lorry from STROUD camp × 30 d 9.2 Sheet 19.5	
	17.9.17		SAILLY 5th Lt INLYS G 22 c 3.8. Sheet 36.	
	19.9.17		38th Div TMB move from SAILLY to HQ CA 6 Sheet 36. X/63 TMB and Z/31 TMB	
CAMP HQCA.6. Sheet 36.			attached to 38th DIV. X, Y, Z and V/Batteries, 38th Division go into the line to take over from the 57th Division.	
	20.9.17		2/Lt E.J. MILLER-WILLIAMS returns from leave to UK.	
	21.9.17		2/Lt J.V. COLLINS and 2/Lt F.BRIGGS return from leave to UK.	
	22.9.17	3-5 am	X/38 shoot on I 21 8 48. 22 Rounds fired 140 hoofgranna 2 Effect Direct hit on trench and parapet. Retaliation heavy 1 OR killed, 1 OR severely and 3 HARRIS	

WAR DIARY
INTELLIGENCE SUMMARY

Army Form C. 2118.

Place	Date	Hour	Summary of Events and Information	Remarks and references to Appendices
CAMP P HQ C.4.6 Sheet 36	22.9.17 (cont)		2/31 fire on C.29.a.40.20 Rounds fired 6. Effect two direct hits Retaliation also on C.29.c.80.75 Rounds fired 3. Prevented from hung mortar by a broken rifle mechanism in each case.	
	23.9.17	3pm	2/38 fire on I.11.a 35.30 Rds fired 1	
	24.9.17	1.45am	2/38 fire on T.16.d.67.65 Rounds fired 30 guns 2. Effect good. Retaliation hand/hvy	
			2/LT MOORE & 2/LT E.J. MILLER-WILLIAMS go into the line	
			X/63 fire on Inconsistent Trench 132.a.71-70 - 132.a.89.98 Rounds fired 30 guns 2. Result good. Retaliation Normal.	
	25.9.17		2/31 fire on Centaur Lane & Trench. Rounds fired 8 Effect Destructive Retaliation Slight	
			also on Central Avenue Rounds fired 6 Effect Destructive Retaliation Slight	
			LT HARRIS and LT GEAGREY return to billets from the line	
	26.9.17		X/63 and Z/31 TM Batteries withdraw to DTMO's HQ at H.9.c.4.6	Appendix 1
	27.9.17		X/63 and Z/31 TM Batteries leave 38th Dn TM's to rejoin their own divisions	
			LT B.V. CLARK goes into the line	
	29.9.17		2/LT W.S. HUNTER and 100 ORs proceed to Reinforcement Camp of SAILLY in order to proceed on 6" Newton Course at Infantry School of Mortars CLARQUES on 30 Sept.	
	30.9.17		DTMO goes to conference at 1st Army School of Mortars.	

O.S. Jones
Captain R.F.A.
38th Dn T.M. Officer

Army Form C. 2118.

WAR DIARY
or
INTELLIGENCE SUMMARY.

(*Erase heading not required.*)

Vol 16

38th Divisional T.M. Battery

October 1917

Army Form C. 2118.

WAR DIARY
or
INTELLIGENCE SUMMARY.
(Erase heading not required.)

Instructions regarding War Diaries and Intelligence Summaries are contained in F.S. Regs., Part II. and the Staff Manual respectively. Title pages will be prepared in manuscript.

Place	Date	Hour	Summary of Events and Information	Remarks and references to Appendices
BIRDCAGE FARM	1/10/17		Lt W.T.O. BONNIWELL relieves 2/Lt E.J MILLER-WILLIAMS in CENTRE GROUP.	
HQC 41.6 FRANCE Sh.36	3/10/17		1 O.R. wounded slightly.	
	6/10/17	3.40 – 5.20	Y/38 fired 14 rounds 9.45" Regulation of DELAPORTE Fm + ORCHARD BARN. Ret. NIL.	
		4 – 5 pm	V/38 fired 12 rounds 9.45" Regulation of STEP Fm	
			Lt W.T.O BONNIWELL and 10 O.R's proceed to 1st Army School of Mortars for course on 6" NEWTON	
	8/10/17		2/Lt W.S. HUNTER relieves Lt B.V. CLARK in LEFT GROUP.	
	9/10/17	12.30 – 2 am	V/38 fired 8 rounds on NED AVENUE in response to SOS V/R BATTERY transferred to V/38 T.M.B.	APPENDIX 1
			V/38 in RIGHT GROUP fired 10 rounds at intervals throughout the day on Delaporte Fm ORCHARD BARN. Ne.of Fm	
			V/38 in LEFT GROUP fired 10 rounds at intervals throughout the day on DEBRIS Fm, CELL RES, CELLLANE	
			V/38 in RIGHT GROUP fired 9 rounds on DELAPORTE Fm + ORCHARD BARN 6 rounds at N.Hall Fm. Heavy retaliation considerable damage to emplacement of C.22.d 50.90	
	12/10/17	3 – 4.45 pm	X/38 fired 9 rounds 2" Target Wire 127 a 00.45 – 127 a 76.30 Result good Ret. Light	
			Y/38 fired 10 rounds throughout the day at NED RES & DELAPORTE Fm. 300 R.b fired at this type DAC +	
	13/10/17	3.15 – 4.45 pm	Z/38 fired 52 rounds 2" Wire 11 a 55.30 – 11 a 50.05 Result good trenches of 38 Sdy Ret Nil Duty	
		6.15 – 9.30 pm	V/38 fired 20 rounds 9.45" Target Wire C.17.c 85.60	
	14/10/17	3.0 – 5.15 pm	V/38 fired 10 rounds at intervals on NED SUPPORT, ORCHARD BARN, DELAPORTE Fm, NED RES	
			X/38 fired 70 rounds 2" 2 guns Target Wire + trenches 121.c.50.15 + 127 a 50.85 Result good effect Retaliation V.Hvy Queer Lit on NoMs	
			Lt G.E.A GREY granted leave to U.K. 3 signallers attacked GTM's in duty on the line.	
	16/10/17	3.25 – 4.0 pm	Z/38 fired 35 rounds 6" NEWTON Target Wire 15 b 20.20 and 13 d 40.90 Result Fair	
		3.0 – 4.45 pm	X/38 fired 78 rounds 2" 2 guns Target Wire 121 C 50.15 Result good Retaliation Hvy heavy	
		3.0 – 4.0 pm	Y/38 fired 49 rounds 2" Target Wire N 11 a 15.55. Result considerable Damage Ret. Slight	
	17/10/17	2.45 – 3.25	V/38 fired 8 rounds 9.45" Regulation of Debris Fm Retaliation nil	

(A7092). Wt W12859/M1293. 75,000. 1/17. D.D. & L., Ltd. Forms/C2118/14.

WAR DIARY
INTELLIGENCE SUMMARY

Army Form C. 2118.

Instructions regarding War Diaries and Intelligence Summaries are contained in F. S. Regs., Part II. and the Staff Manual respectively. Title pages will be prepared in manuscript.

(Erase heading not required.)

Place	Date	Hour	Summary of Events and Information	Remarks and references to Appendices
BIRDCAGE FM. HQC4 G FRANCE SH36.	18/10/17	5:15 – 4:45pm 3:30 – 5:10pm	V/38 fired 20 rounds 9.45" Registration of NEO FM (N 11.c 80.30) 4 direct hits	
	19/10/17	2:20 – 4:0pm	X/38 fired 40 rounds 6" Newton Target B Battery (127b) good effect. Retaliation heavy 10 cm Howr 4 HTTM Z/38 fired 90 rounds 6" Target Wire 15d 30.80 – 15d 40.97 Wire & stakes blown up	
	20/10/17	3:0 – 3:25-230pm 4:15-4:5pm 3 – 3:30	W/38 fired 20 rounds 9.45" Target NEO FARM 4 hits. N/38 fired 8 rounds 9.45" on DEBRIS FM. Retaliation Heavy Detachment shower from guns. V/38 fired 9 rounds 9.45" Target HTM at C17aS2 + C17d32.62. Y/36 fired 21 rounds 2" Wire N11a9.95. Result Clean gap cut. Retaliation Slight	
		3 – 3:40 3:10 – 4:15	V/38 fired 31 rounds 6" Newton Target Wire N6b65.20 Knot knife not wires cut Z/38 fired 52 rounds 6" Newton Target Wire 15 b2.52– good effect	different
	21/10/17	2:30 – 4:0 1:30 – 2:0pm 2:0 – 3:30	LT G.G. HARRIS REA relieved 2/LT E.F MILLER WILLIAMS in CENTRE GROUP. LT B.V CLARK relieved 3/LT W.S HULETT V/38 fired 86 rounds 6" Newton Target Wire N6b60.15. Retaliation from 10.15cm tm X/38 fired 22 rounds 2" Target Wire 12.16b60.15 X/38 fired 13 rounds 6" Target Distillery 127b. Retaliation very heavy enemy target changes unaltered	
		3:10 – 4:15	Z/38 fired 40 rounds 2" Target Wire C29c60.60 – C29d05.20 Considerable damage done	
	22/10/17	3:30 – 4:5pm 2:0 – 2:40	V/38 fired 7 rounds 9.45" Target Naval Avenue Nodirect hits Y/38 fired 32 rounds 6" Target Wire N6b60.18 Clean gap formed Retaliation Slight	
	23/10/17		X/38 fired 4 rounds on D Battery (127b) 6"	
	24/10/17	2:20 – 3:40pm 3:10 – 4:15pm	Y/36 fired 36 rounds 6" Target Wire N6b65.18 – N6b62.20 2 clean gaps formed Retaliation heavy Burst short Y/38 fired 30 rounds 6" Target W62 MACQUART Result Good	
		2:30 – 3:50	Z/38 fired 65 rounds 2" Target Wire C29c60.60 – C29d05.30 About 2/3 destruction on wire	
	25/10/17	2:30 – 4:15pm	LT G.A GREY Returns from leave, UK Z/38 fire 62 rounds 6" Target wire 15d25.30 – 15d30.80 Small gap not visible	

(A7092). Wt. W12539/M1293. 75,000. 1/17. D. D. & L., Ltd. Forms/C.2118/14.

Army Form C. 2118.

WAR DIARY
or
INTELLIGENCE SUMMARY.
(Erase heading not required.)

Instructions regarding War Diaries and Intelligence Summaries are contained in F. S. Regs., Part II. and the Staff Manual respectively. Title pages will be prepared in manuscript.

Place	Date	Hour	Summary of Events and Information	Remarks and references to Appendices
BIRDCAGE F.M. HQ 4.6	25/10/17	2.0 – 3.0 p.m.	Y/38 TMB fired 26 rounds 6" Newton Target N6d 50.85. Retaliation Heavy, 1 m. buried	
FRANCES 26.36.	26/10/17	3.0 – 4.20 a.m.	X/38 TMB fired 80 rounds 2" Target wire I22.a.20.15 – I22.a.40.43 Retaliation Slight	
		3.0 – 3.55 a.m.	V/38 TMB fired 12 rounds 9.45" Target Cell Support + direct hits on Trench	
	27/10/17	1.0 am	Y/38 fired 27 rounds 6" Newton on O1a 10.65, O1a 15.74, O1a 29.85 cooperation with Artillery in raid. Heavy retaliation. 1 O.R. wounded	
		3.30 – 4.30 pm	Z/38 fired 30 rounds 6" Target C23c 75.70 Good results. No retaliation, all OK	
	28/10/17	11 – 11.30 am	X/38 fired 40 rounds 6" Target Include Support I21d 00.30 Heavy retaliation	
		4 – 4.5 pm	V/38 fired 10 rounds 9.45" Target Junction of Celt Row + Celt Trench	
	29/10/17	1.40 – 2.20 pm	Z/38 fired 133 rounds 6" Target I11a 55.80 + I11a 40.30 Three gaps observed in wire Retaliation slight	
	30/17	11 am – 1 pm, 4 pm – 4.30	2/Lt R.H. DEWHIRST proceeds on leave to UK	
		12.30 – 1.30 pm	X/38 fired 26 rounds 6" Newton Target Include Support I21c 93.23 – I21d 20.55 Ret. Heavy	
		2.30 – 4.0 pm	Z/38 fired 95 rounds 6" Target Wire I5 c 65.05 – I11 a 40.30 Considerable damage Ret. Slight	
	31/10/17	10.15 – 11.45 pm	V/38 fired 15 rounds 9.45" Target Front Line N11a 20.85. Retaliation Normal. 2 O.R. wounded.	
		12 – 4.0 pm	Z/38 fired 149 rounds 6" Newton Target wire I5 c 65.05 – I11 a 40.30. Several gaps observed.	

O J Jones
Captain R.F.A.
D.T.M.O. 38th Div.

Army Form C. 2118.

WAR DIARY
or
INTELLIGENCE SUMMARY.
(Erase heading not required.)

38th Divisional T.M. Batteries

NOVEMBER 1917

Army Form C. 2118.

WAR DIARY
or
INTELLIGENCE SUMMARY.
(Erase heading not required.)

Instructions regarding War Diaries and Intelligence Summaries are contained in F. S. Regs., Part II. and the Staff Manual respectively. Title pages will be prepared in manuscript.

Place	Date	Hour	Summary of Events and Information	Remarks and references to Appendices
BIRDCAGE FM HQ 4.6 FRANCE Sheet 36	1/1/17	11.30–1.0 am	Z/38 fired 114 rounds 6" Newton Target Wire 15 c 65.05 – I 11 a 40.30. Heavy retaliation on PORT EGAL AVENUE.	
		3.0–3.30	V/38 fired 5 rounds 9·45" Target CELL RESERVE. Visibility too bad for further shooting	Ditto instructions APPENDIX 2
			Lt G.E.A. GREY goes up to LEFT GROUP, handing over V/38 to 2/Lt MOORE, to assist Lt CLARK in bombard with a detachment of 5 men.	
	2/1/17	2.30–4.0 am	V/38 fired 15 rounds 9·45" Target NED AVENUE, NED RESERVE, NED FARM. 6 direct hits.	
		2.30–3.30 am	30 rounds 6" Newton Target NIG as 121 G 50.30. Trench damaged.	
		2.30–3.0 pm	X/38 fired 15 rounds 6" Newton Target INCLUDE SUPPORT 121 d 10.50 fired to draw retaliation and conceal the other gun. Retaliation heavy.	
		2.0–3.5 am	Z/38 fired 40 rounds 6" Newton Target Wire 15 c 65.05 – 11 a 40.30 Good effect	
		3.15–4.0 am	Patrol under Lt GREY fired 80 rounds 6" Newton Target C 23 a 75.10 – C 23 C 80.70 Visibility very bad. Wire + stakes thrown up.	
			Lt W.T.O. BONNIWELL leaves X 38 TMB on transfer to 63rd Divisional Artillery.	
	3/1/17	2.0–2.20	L/GREY in LEFT SECTOR fired 90 rounds 6" Newton Target C 23 a 70.10 to C 23 C 80.70	
		2.5–4.0 am	Z/38 fired 129 rounds 6" Newton Target Wire 15 c 65.05 to 11 a 40.30 Considerable damage done. Retaliation heavy.	
		8.30 am–9.30 am	Heavy Trench Mortar position at C 22 K 45.95 bombarded by hostile TM's. One ShLt in pit which has been put in action for some time became. Casualties – 2 O.R's wounded	
	4/1/17	2.0–3.30 am	Lt GREY in LEFT SECTOR fired 82 rounds 6" Newton Target Wire C 23 a 70.10 – C 23 c 90.70.	
		2.30–4.0 am	Z/38 TMB fired 132 rounds 6" Newton Target Wire 15 c 60.65 to 11 a 40.30 4 hits on TMs During this shoot hostile TM at 15 A 55.50 been engaged and silenced	
	5/1/17	2.45–4.0 am	Lt GREY in LEFT SECTOR fired 100 rounds 6" Newton Target Wire C 23 a 70.10 – C 23 c 90.70 Considerable damage. Retaliation slight	

Army Form C. 2118.

WAR DIARY
or
INTELLIGENCE SUMMARY.
(Erase heading not required.)

Place	Date	Hour	Summary of Events and Information	Remarks and references to Appendices
BIRDCAGE F.M.E. HqC.A.6	5/11/17	2.15–4.0 am	Z/38 T.M.B. fired 70 rounds 6" NEWTON Target Wire 15cGO.10 – 111a40.30 Barrage cut 20 yards.	
		2.20–4.0 am	Z/38 T.M.B. fired 17 rounds 6" NEWTON Target Wire 15cGO.10 – 111a40.30 Direct hit on dugout at 111a60.70. Retaliation slight.	
	6/11/17	2.10–2.20 am	Z/38 T.M.B. fired 20 rounds 6" NEWTON Target trench + wire 122 a 92.93. Target registered.	
		12.0–12.35 pm	L/GREY in LEFT SECTOR fired 55 rounds 6" NEWTON Target Wire C23 c80.70. Wire very badly damaged.	
		12.0–3.0 pm	Z/38 T.M.B. fired 129 rounds 6" NEWTON Target Wire 15cGO.05 – 111a AD.30 Minnie at 111c 95.50 silenced during this shoot. Our wire apparently cut on last night.	
	7/11/17	12.0–3.0 pm	Z/38 T.M.B. fired 73 rounds 6" NEWTON Target Wire 15cGO.05 – 111a40.30 cleared.	TM11/98 Left Inf. D.&C.2025/DIV. Enclopho "BB29" 2.
		12.30–1.50 pm	A/GREY in LEFT SECTOR fired 30 rounds 6" NEWTON Target CENSORS NOSE Wire appears to be cut completely.	
		2.10–2.45 pm	V/38 fired 10 rounds 9.45" Target 121d 28.70 Target registered	
	8/11/17	RAID by 13th RWF Artillery shooting :- 19.45" TM, 36" Newton TM, 12" TM		
			V/38 fired 7 rounds 9.45" Target 1.21.d.28.70 } Time 1.24 a.m. – 1.54 a.m.	
			X/38 fired 15 rounds 2" Target 1.16.d.03.22	
			X/38 fired 145 rounds 6" NEWTON Targets (3 guns) 1.16 d.49.48, 22 a 53.77, 21 & 55.22	
		RAID by 15th RWF & 10th SWB	RAID by 10th & SWB Artillery shooting 3 6" NEWTON TMs Z/38 fired 285 rounds 6" NEWTON Targets (3 guns) Minnie at 111c 95.55 MG at 15 & 15.30 } Time 1.24 a.m. – 2.55 a.m. CENSORS NOSE	TM11/98 APPENDIX 2.
	9/11/17		Personnel of V/38 attached to X/38 returns to Right Sector. 2 Lt. Cumbo RE returns to billet. Lieut. G.E.A. GREY + detachment of V/38 attached to Z/38 come out of the line.	

Army Form C. 2118.

WAR DIARY
or
INTELLIGENCE SUMMARY.
(Erase heading not required.)

Instructions regarding War Diaries and Intelligence Summaries are contained in F. S. Regs., Part II. and the Staff Manual respectively. Title pages will be prepared in manuscript.

Place	Date	Hour	Summary of Events and Information	Remarks and references to Appendices
BIRDCAGE FARM. 49c 4.6. France Sheet 36	9/11/17	3.0 – 4.0 pm	Lt B.V. CLARK + one THIRD of Z/38 TMB come out of the line. One THIRD of X/38 TMB return to Billets	TM1/1/95 APPENDIX 2
	10/11/17		Z/38 T.M.B. fire 50 rounds 6" NEWTON TARGET Coy HQ 111a91·80. Timber thrown up.	
	11/17	2.0 – 3.20 pm	V/38 T.M.B. fired 20 rounds 9·45" TARGET Hostile TM 121 b 65·00	
		3.25 – 4.0 pm	X/38 T.M.B. fired 40 rounds 6" Target. Trench and wire 122 a 10·36. Considerable damage done	
		3.30 – 4.0 pm	X/38 T.M.B. fired 30 rounds 6" TARGET Trench and wire 116 d 15·30 Damage to wire & trench	
	12/17	8.0 – 8.15 am	Z/38 T.M.B. fired 15 rounds 6" TARGET Censor's Nose. Retaliation for hostile Bombardment.	
			X/38 T.M.B. move their Headquarters to MOAT FARM, BOIS GRENIER	
			Lt B.V. CLARK relieves 2/Lt W.S. HUNTER in LEFT GROUP.	
	13/17	2.30 – 3.0 pm	Z/38 T.M.B. fired 4 rounds 2" TARGET C29C 60·60 Gun shooting invariably but one small hit	
		2.30 – 3.10 pm	X/38 TMB fired 20 rounds 6" TARGET INCLUDE SUPPORT. 121 c 98·32. Heavy retaliation on Inf.	
		2.45 – 3.30 pm	X/38 T.M.B. fired 30 rounds 6" TARGET DUGOUTS at 115 & 90·06 Target observed by mortar of trench.	
	14/17	3.20 – 4.0 pm	Z/38 T.M.B. had 21 rounds 6" TARGET Censor's Nose. C23 central. Retaliation for 4 hostile HTM rounds	
			Lt G.G. HARRIS relieves 2 Lt E.J. MILLER-WILLIAMS in the line. CONFERENCE held at 113 Bde HQ on subject of TRENCH MORTARS.	APPENDIX 3a
			Z/38 excavate for placing new dugouts as their headquarters subsidiary line.	
	15/17	2.10 – 3.0 pm	Z/38 fired 35 rounds 6" TARGET CENSOR's NOSE. Wire cutting. Observation dug-out.	
			Capt L.W. FOX M.C. gun list granted leave to U.K.	
	16/17	1.55 – 3.0 pm	V/38 TMB. fired 11 rounds 9·45" TARGET Hostile T.M. at C29 a 80·20. Three hits on trench near entrance	
		2.30 – 3.0 pm	V/38 TMB fired 5 rounds 9·45" TARGET Dugouts at 121 b 95·05. Two hits on trench.	

Army Form C. 2118.

WAR DIARY
or
INTELLIGENCE SUMMARY.

(Erase heading not required.)

Instructions regarding War Diaries and Intelligence Summaries are contained in F.S. Regs., Part II. and the Staff Manual respectively. Title pages will be prepared in manuscript.

Place	Date	Hour	Summary of Events and Information	Remarks and references to Appendices
BIRDCAGE FARM HQ 4 G Frise Shelts	16th/17	5.0pm	Z/38 TMB fired 15 rounds 6" Newton Target C23d 22.70 Retaliation for Hostile TM	
		5.0pm	Z/38 TMB fired 8 rounds 6" Target I5b 60.00 Retaliation for Hostile TM fire	
		2.0pm–2.45	X/38 TMB fired 19 rounds 6" Target Dugouts at I21c 60.45	
		2.0pm–2.45	X/38 TMB fired 50 rounds 6" Target Dugouts at I22a 60.50	
		2.30–3.0pm	Y/38 TMB fired 15 rounds 6" Target Hostile wire O1a 10.65 Retaliation. Wire effective	
	17/17	2.05–2.55pm	Z/38 TMB fired 26 rounds 6" Target Hostile wire C23d 76.45 Retaliation	
		3.0pm	Z/38 TMB fired 20 rounds 6" Target C23d 25.70 Retaliation for Hostile TM fire	
		1.0–2.0pm	V/38 TMB fired 15 rounds 9.45" Target I21b 95.10 three rounds effective on wire	
		1.30pm	Z/38 TMB fired 15 rounds 6" Target C23d 20.70 Retaliation for Hostile TM fire	
	18th/17	11.0–12.0am	"Z"/38 TMB fired 10 rounds 6" Target Inane Drive. Retaliation for Hostile TM Fire	
	19th/17	2.15–2.55pm	V/38 TMB fired 9 rounds 9.45" Target Centaur Reg. + Centaur Support 2 hits on trench	
		10.45–11.15am	Z/38 TMB fired 20 rounds 6" Target C23c 70.70 Retaliation for Hostile HTM fire.	
		2.40–3.0pm	Z/38 TMB fired 27 rounds 6" Target C29c 40.90 + C29c 90.40 Retaliation	
		3.0–4.0pm	X/38 TMB fired 50 rounds 16" Targets Dugout I22a 40.62 Post I22a 62.78	
		2.45–3.0pm	X/38 TMB fired 20 rounds 6" Targets Dugout I21c 80.45 Very heavy retaliation was caused	

My Uncles.

10 Officers (Hon. H.G. Poynter) and 45 OR's report to Birdcage Farm for duty with 38th Div T.M.s
Capt. Noel V/R TMB remains with 1st Portuguese Divisional Artillery.
LT BUCLARK relieves LT WS Hunter in Left Group.

Army Form C. 2118.

WAR DIARY
or
INTELLIGENCE SUMMARY.
(Erase heading not required.)

Instructions regarding War Diaries and Intelligence Summaries are contained in F. S. Regs., Part II. and the Staff Manual respectively. Title pages will be prepared in manuscript.

Place	Date	Hour	Summary of Events and Information	Remarks and references to Appendices
BIRDCAGE Fm H9c 4.6 France Sh36	20th/17	at intervals throughout the day	Z/38 TMB fired 23 rounds 6" Target C23 d 20.70	Retaliation for Hostile TM fire
			Z/38 TMB fired 20 rounds 6" Target C29 d 05.90	
			Z/38 TMB fired 30 rounds 6" Target 15h 70.00	
	21st/17	at intervals throughout the day	Z/38 TMB fired 19 rounds 6" Target 11h 95.90	
			Z/38 TMB fired 35 rounds 6" Target C29 a 50.05, C29 a 34.67	Retaliation for Hostile TM fire
			Z/38 TMB fired 15 Rounds 6" Target C23 d 20.70	
			38 TMD Divisional TMB S.O.S. orders issued to LEFT and CENTRE GROUPS	APPENDIX 6
		1.30-2.45pm	X/38 TMB fired 75 rounds 6" Target Dugouts at C22 a 40.62 + C22 a 62.78 Effective shoot	
	22nd/17	throughout the day	Z/38 TMB fired 43 rounds 6" Target 11h 05.90	
			Z/38 TMB fired 20 rounds 6" Target C29 d 34.67	Retaliation for Hostile TM Fire
			Z/38 TMB fired 33 rounds 6" Target C23 d 20.70	
	23rd/17	1.15-2.0pm	Y/38 TMB fired 12 rounds 9.45 Target. CENSUS TR + CENSUS ROW 3 H.G on trench	
		2.10-3.40	Z/38 TMB fired 12 rounds 6" Target 11h C 52.79 + 11 a 32.30	Regulation
			1 O.R. of V/38 TMB wounded.	
	24th/17	5.15-5.30am	2/38 TMB fired 20 rounds 6" Target C29 d 20.09	Retaliation for Hostile fire
		5.15-6.0am	2/38 TMB fired 32 rounds 6" Target C23 d 80.60	S.O.S.
		1.30-3.0pm	X/38 TMB fired 40 rounds 6" Target 122 d 70.35	Material blown up
		1.30-3.0pm	X/38 TMB fired 40 rounds 6" Target 122 a 40.62 + 122 d 62.78	Parapets knocked down & corner of dugout exposed

(A7092). W1 W1259/M1293 75,000. 1/17. D. D. & L., Ltd. Forms/C.2118/14.

Army Form C. 2118.

WAR DIARY
or
INTELLIGENCE SUMMARY.
(Erase heading not required.)

Instructions regarding War Diaries and Intelligence Summaries are contained in F. S. Regs., Part II. and the Staff Manual respectively. Title pages will be prepared in manuscript.

Place	Date	Hour	Summary of Events and Information	Remarks and references to Appendices
BIRDCAGE FARM HQ C.6. R.ES 36 France	24/11/17	5am	The bombers of CENTRAL AVENUE 6" emplacement blown in during hostile bombardment. 1 wounded.	
	25/11/17	1.0 – 2.30pm	Z/38 T.M.B. fired 6 rounds 6" Target INANE DRIVE. High explosive accurate shot. 1 N.C.O. Z/38 TMB wounded in action (CPL GOLDSBY). L/S G. HARRIS RFA slightly wounded, not serious, remained at duty. AMENDMENT to notes on CONFERENCE of 14.11.17 received.	APPENDIX 3(?)
	26/11/17	1.55 – 2.55pm	V/38 TMB. fired 17 rounds 9.45" Target MINNIE C.29.b.80.95. 3 Direct hits on trench.	
		2.15 – 2.30pm	X/38 TMB fired 10 rounds 6" Target 12.1.d.17.52. Material Unknown	
		2.50 – 3.18pm	X/38 TMB fired 40 rounds 6" Target 1.22.a.50.45	
		2.30 – 2.32pm	Z/38 TMB fired 5 rounds 6" Target (29.d.50.00)	
		3.10 – 3.15pm	Z/38 TMB fired 10 rounds 6" Target C.23.d.22.67 § Retaliation for hostile T.M. fire.	
			LT G G HARRIS proceeded on leave to UK.	
			CAPT NOEL transferred to 212th TMB duty to be detailed 2nd/Div. 1 OR wounded	
	27/11/17	2.0 – 3.0pm	/38 TMB fired 103 rounds 6" Target NEAR SUPPORT & INDEX SUPPORT. 7 details unrecovered in hostile trench, small dump destroyed.	APPENDIX A
			38 SOS's normal SOS orders for TMB issued to RIGHT GROUP	
	28/11/17	1.0 – 1.25pm	V/38 TMB fired 8 rounds 9.45" Target 121 b.60.10 much material thrown up.	
		1.0 – 2.10pm	X/38 TMB fired 80 rounds 6" Target INCLINE SUPPORT. Heavy slabs of iron with 10 sec. fuse.	
		1.0 – 2.0pm	X/38 TMB fired 60 rounds 6" Target INCLINE SUPPORT. High wind.	
		2.0 – 2.45pm	Z/38 TMB fired 34 rounds 6" Target CENSOR SUPPORT. Heavy retaliation. 1 detachment withdrawn from the gun.	
			1 OR of Z/38 TMB wounded in action.	

Army Form C. 2118.

WAR DIARY
or
INTELLIGENCE SUMMARY.
(Erase heading not required.)

Instructions regarding War Diaries and Intelligence Summaries are contained in F. S. Regs., Part II. and the Staff Manual respectively. Title pages will be prepared in manuscript.

Place	Date	Hour	Summary of Events and Information	Remarks and references to Appendices
BIROCAGE FM HQ4 6 FRANCESTHAL 38.	28/11/17		2/Lt CH MOORE relieves Lt GEA GREY in the Right Sector 2/Lt HUNTER gassed returns to lie.	
	29/11/17	2.0pm	Z/38 TMB moves Main Headquarters to TISSAGE in HOUPLINES. V/38 TMB fired 6 rounds 9.45" target DELANGRE FARM.	
		2.30–3.45pm	X/38 TMB fired 50 rounds 6" target at 116 d 52.97. Wire knocked at 116 d 55 yx.	
			INFANTRY OFFICER from 113 Bde started GX/38 TMB to liaison officer	
	30/11/17	3.20–4.20pm	X/38 TMB fired 100 rounds 6" Target 121 d 40.70 – 121 b 6500 considerable damage done.	
		1.0– 1.15pm	V/38 TMB fired 3 rounds 9.45" Target CENTAUR SUPPORT C.29c.	
		1.20– 1.35pm	V/38 TMB fired 4 rounds 9.45" Target CENTAUR ROW C.29a.	
		2.20– 3.5pm	V/38 TMB fired 10 rounds 9.45" Target Junction of INCENSE SUPP & INCENSE AVENUE 17X	

O Stone
Capt RFA
DTMO 38th Division

R.A., 38th DIVISION No. G.S.439

O.C.,
    Right Group.
    Centre Group.
    Left Group.
    D.T.M.O.

At a Conference held at the 113th Brigade H.Q's on 14th 11-1917, the following decisions were made, with regard to working of Trench Mortars in the line.

The following were present:-

G.O.C. 113th Infantry Brigade.
G.O.C., 114th Infantry Brigade.
G.O.C., 115th Infantry Brigade.
C.R.A.
C.R.E.
Group Commanders.
D.T.M.O.
T.M.Battery Commanders.
O's C Field Coy's R.E.

1. Work on Emplacements

(a) The Trench Mortar Battery Commander of the Sector concerned to be responsible for all the work in the Sector.

(b) R.E., to be consulted as to the Technical details of design and a plan, of the work, estimate of the material and men-hours required & drawn up by the Field Coy R.E. Commander before the work is started

(c) D.T.M.O., to apply to the Infantry Brigadier for the working paeties he requires. These parties to be found by the Battalion holding the Subsidiary line, and to consist as a rule of 1 N.C.O. and 6 men per emplacement under construction. The men detailed should be changed as seldom as possible.

(d) An Infantry Officer of the Battalion finding the working parties to visit the work at least once daily, to ensure that the men are being usefully employed.

(e) An R.E., man to be permanently employed on each Emplacement, or, failing this, a man from the T.M.Battery. These men should not be changed if it can be possibly avoided.

(f) The construction of certain emplacements wholly in the hands of the R.E.

(g) Liaison between T.M., personnel and the R.E., to be improved. Cases have been reported when R.E., have not been informed that work could not be carried on certain days.

2. Tactical controll

(a) Brigadiers to deal direct with D,T,M.O., or his representative. Brigadiers will issue all Orders regarding what objectives they wish to be engaged by Trench Mortars, and the number of rounds they wish to be fired. These Orders should be issued direct to Batteries or through the D.T.M.O.,
Group Commanders will arrange to give covering fire to T.M's when required.

(b) Sites for T.M.Emplacements to be selected by the D.T.M.O., and submitted to the Brigadiers concerned for approval.

(c) Emplacements to be sited as far as possible, near tramlines or roads. Main communications trenches to be avoided.

(d) For the purposes of S.O.S., Liaison to be direct between Coy., H.Q's and the guns in the Coy., Sector.

3. Infantry Liaison with T.M.Batteries

One Infantry Officaer to be attached to T.M.Batteries (1 per Battery) for periods of a week to 10 days, to encourage mutual co-operation between Infantry and T.M's.

SECRET.

R.A. 38/th. Div. No. G.S. 501
38/th. Div. No. G.S.S. 9/2

38/th. Div. Arty.

With reference to the Conference held on 14-11-17, with reference to the working of Trench Mortars in the line.

The Major General does not agree with Para. 2 - (a) TACTICAL CONTROL - and directs me to forward his remarks thereon:-

"The Trench Mortars are part and parcel of the Divis-"ional Artillery and are not to be separated. Tactically they are "generally used or ought to be used in conjunction with the guns. "Consequently they should be controlled by the Group Commander. It "is just as easy for Brigadiers to issue their orders regarding what "they require in fact easier as they deal direct with one responsible "person and the conjunction of the guns and the Trench Mortars is "ensured at the same time".

With the exception of Para 2 - (a) the G.O.C. approves the minutes of the Conference.

25-11-17.

(Signed) J.E. MUNBY, LT. Colonel.
General Staff, 38/th. (Welsh) Division.

~~Appendix 1~~
APPENDIX 2

38th Div TMB WAR DIARY

Nov. 1917

T.M. 1/95.

115 Infantry Brigade.
Left Artillery Group.
Z/38/T.M.B.
Y/38/T.M.B.

      One Officer and One 6" NEWTON detachment of Y/38th. T.M.B. will move into Left Group on the morning of the 2nd. inst. in order to carry out a Trench Mortar Demonstration against CENSORS NOSE. This demonstration will commence on the afternoon of the 2nd. inst. Every effort will be made to make it as effective as possible. If hostile retaliation against the Trench Mortar Emplacement at C.22.d.25.60. prevents an effective demonstration from being made, the detachment of Y/38/T.M.B. will proceed to carry out a demonstration against CENTRAL TRENCH C.29.c. with a 2" Trench Mortar firing from I.4.b.95.95.

1-11-17.

Captain R.F.A.,
D.T.M.O., 38/th. Division.

War Diary

APPENDIX 2

T.M. 1/98.

SECRET.

O.C. X/38/T.M.B.
    Z/38/T.M.B.
    V/38/T.M.B.

With reference to the operations on the night of the 7/8th inst.

1. ZERO hour will be notified later by special orderly.

2. 2/Lieut T.F.BRIGGS., R.F.A., will synchronise watches for Batteries in the Line. Synchronised time will be sent up by an orderly leaving D.T.M.O's., H.Q., at 4-0 pm.

3. The signal for T.M's., opening fire will be the commencement of the Artillery barrage. On no account are any T.M's., to open fire before the Artillery.

4. Operation orders are forwarded herewith. These orders will be returned to this Office on completion of the Operation.

5. No orders have yet been received from the Artillery Groups. These will be forwarded as soon as they arrive.

6. If the wind is favourable No. 1. Special Coy R.E., will discharge gas at ZERO hour on C.29.a.,b.,and c., and on I.16.b., and d. In the event of the wind being unfavourable for the discharge, the code word "CHICAGO" will be sent out. All detachments in the Front Line will wear their box respirators from ZERO minus 5 to ZERO plus 15.

7. On completion of the Operation, the personnel of "Y" Battery attached to "X" Battery will return to their own sector 2/Lieut C.H.MOORE., R.F.A and the detachment which proceeded from billets will return to billets. On the morning of the 8th inst., the following will move out of the Line. :-
   Lieut GREY R.F.A. and detachment of "Y" attached to "Z"
   Lieut CLARK R.F.A. and one third of "Z" Battery.
   One third of "X" Battery.

Captain R.F.A.
D.T.M.O. 38th Division.

6-11-17.

S E C R E T.

LEFT GROUP :- 36th Div. Artillery. Operation Order No.3
November 6th, 1917

1. The 10th Batt. S.W. Borderers is raiding the enemy in INCANDESCENT TRENCH and SUPPORT tomorrow night 7/8th Nov. Zero hour will be notified later.

The Raiding Party will be formed in NO MAN'S LAND, just in front of our own wire by Zero hour.

The points of entry are between I.11.a.45.32 and I.5.c.70.05. and after the entry has been effected, Blocks are being established at the following points viz :-

I.11.a.83.25.
I.11.a.60.37.
I.11.b.08.80.
I.11.b.02.85.
I.5.c.70.05.

and flanking parties in NO MAN's LAND at
I.11.a.28.32.
I.5.c.60.12.

~~xxxxxxxxxxxxxxxxxxxxxxxxxxxxxxxxxxxxxxxxxxxxxxxxxx
Creeping Barrage~~

2. The Left Group Artillery programme and one amendment thereto have been issued to all concerned.

Special care is to be taken that the first lift of the Creeping barrage shall be far enough beyond the enemy front line to allow of the raiders climbing out of the front trench on their way to the Support Line.

3. The Left Group M.T.M's will co-operate with one 6" Newton gun each on a suspected T.M. at I.11.c.95.50; a suspected M.G. at I.5.b.25.25.; and CENSORS NOSE.

4. The following O.P's will be manned by an Officer found as shown against them, on the night 7/8th Nov. from Zero - 1 Hour until the order "Break off" is given from this Office, when normal night manning will be resumed viz:-
EREHWON or NOWHERE by A/121.
BRENTWOOD by D/121.

5. Liaison Officers will be found as follows on the night 7/8th Nov.-
Right Battalion Headquarters...D/121.
Right Battalion Advanced Headquarters at Centre Co. Headquarters
I.10.b.50.85..........B/121.
Left Battalion Headquarters....C/121.
An experienced Officer is to be sent in each case.

The Liaison Officers with Right Battalion will keep Left Group R.A. informed as to the progress of the Operation; reports of hostile shelling are of the utmost importance, and will be sent in by Liaison Officers and O.P's as it occurs.

An Officer from Group Headquarters is being sent to O.P. Exchange during the Operation.

APPENDIX 3 (a & b)

38th Dival TMB WAR DIARY

NOV. 1917

SECRET.   C.G.652
                                                                 Copy No.

CENTRE GROUP, 38TH. DIVISIONAL ARTILLERY OPERATION ORDER NO. 29.

                                                    November 7th. 1917.

1.   On the night of the 7/8th. November at an hour to be notified
later a party of the 14th Battn., R.W.F., will enter the enemy's
Front Line at I.22.a.26.53. and attack the enemy post reported
to be at that place.

2.   The strength of the party will be 1 Officer, 6 N.C.Os. and 31
Other ranks.
        The party will be commanded by 2/Lt. H.G.ROBERTS, 13th. Bn.,
R.W.F.

3.   Centre Group Artillery will co-operate as follows :-

                                Guns.   Trench Mortars.

                         18-pr.   4.5"How.   6"   2"   9.45"

378th. Battery :-   6
C/332.   "   2.
X/38. L.T.M.Bty :-   3   1
V/38. H.T.M. " :-   1

4.   At ZERO minus 1 min. the Infantry Party will rush the sentry
and attack the post.
        At ZERO guns and Trench Mortars will open simultaneously on
the following points (see attached tracing) :-

378th. Bty.   6 guns   .. INCLEMENT SUPPORT from I.22.a.50.47.
                                                    to I.22.a.16.10.
C/332. Bty.   1 How. .. I.22.a.70.60.
                   1 How. .. I.21.b.95.03.
X/38.M.T.M.Bty.   1 6" T.M. I.16.d.40.48.
                   1 do.   I.22.a.53.77.
                   1 do.   I.21.b.55.22.
                   1 2" T.M. I.16.d.03.22.
V/38.H.T.M.Bty.   1 9.45"TM. I.21.a.28.70.

        2" Stokes Mortars and Machine guns will also co-operate.

5.   Rate of fire will be as follows :-

18-Pdrs.

        ZERO to ZERO plus 4   4 rds. per gun per min.   96.
        ZERO plus 4 to ZERO plus 10.   3 rds. per gun per min.   108.
        ZERO plus 10 to ZERO plus 20. 2 rds. per gun per min.   120.
        ZERO plus 20 to ZERO plus 30. 1 rd. per gun per min.   60.

                                                                  384

4.5". Hows:

        ZERO to ZERO plus 10.   2 rds. per gun per min.   40.
        ZERO plus 10 to ZERO plus 30. 1 rd. per gun per min.   40.

                                                                   80

TRENCH MORTARS.

        ZERO to ZERO plus 10.   Intense.
        ZERO plus 10 to ZERO plus 30. Moderate rate, gradually
                                            slowing down.

.2.

6. 378 Battery will detail an Officer to be at SIGNAL BOX O.P. during the Raid. He will report at this O.P. one hour before ZERO.

7. Gas will be discharged at ZERO on to the enemy's lines in the vicinity of WIM ACQURT by No. 1 Special Company R.E.

In the event of the wind being unfavourable the following code word will be sent :-

CHICAGO.

8. Watches will be synchronised by representatives of Batteries at Centre Group Headquarters at 7 p.m. on the night of 7/8th November.

9. ACKNOWLEDGE.

R Kash
Capt. R.F.A.
Adjutant, Centre Group,
38th. Divisional Artillery.

Issued at   a.m.

Copy No. 1. War Diary.
"   2. File.
     3. 377 Battery.
     4. 378 Battery.
     5. C/332. Battery.
     6. X/38. M.T.M.Battery.
     7. V/38. H.T.M.Battery.
     8. 38th. Divisional Artillery.
     9. 113th. Infantry Brigade.
    10. 13th. Battalion R. W. F.
    11. Left Artillery Group.
    12. Right Artillery Group.
    13. D.T.M.O., 38th Division.
    14.
    15.
    16.

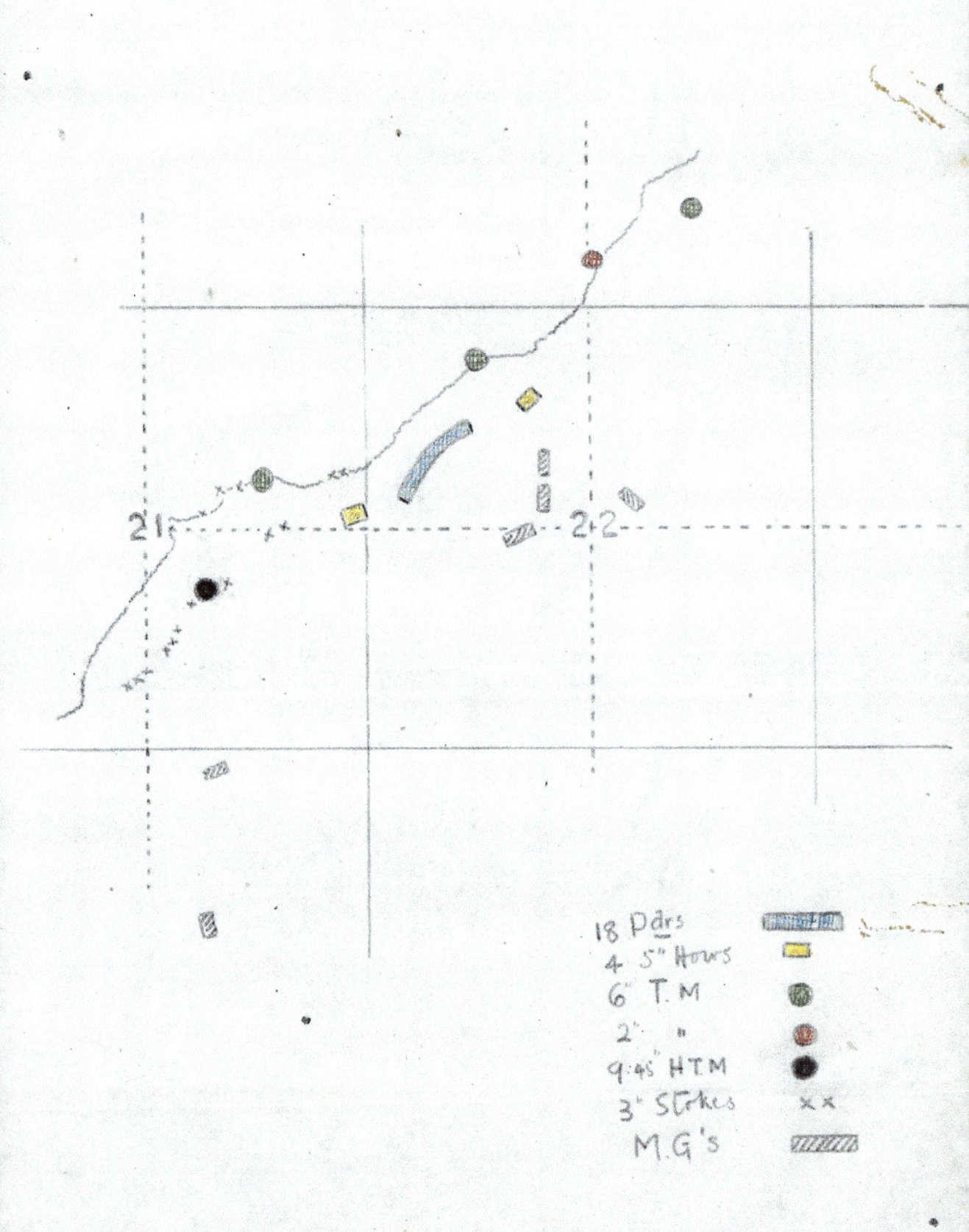

APPENDIX 4.

38th Dvnl T.M.B. WAR DIARY.

NOV 1917.

S E C R E T.
XXXXXXXXXXX

38th. DIVISIONAL TRENCH MORTAR BATTERIES.

S.O.S. ORDERS - RIGHT GROUP.

1. 6" Newtom T.M's will be manned by night as far as possible in order to strengthen the Artillery "S.O.S" Barrages.

2. The Group is divided into "S.O.S" Sectors as follows :-

"A"	-	N. 8.d. 3. 1.	to	N. 9.c.46.04.
"B"	-	N. 9.c.46.04.	to	N. 9.d.68.18.
"C"	-	N. 9.d.68.18.	to	N.10.d.13.65.
"D"	-	N.10.d.13.65.	to	N.11.a.05.50.
"E"	-	N.11.a.05.50.	to	N. 5.d.35.21.
"F"	-	N. 5.d.35.21.	to	N. 6.c.89.56.
"G"	-	N. 6.c.89.56.	to	N. 6.b.86.35.
"H"	-	N. 6.b.86.35.	to	I. 31.c.75.00.

3. Each gun will have a separate "S.O.S" target for each Sector. These targets are selected points in or near the enemy's front line wire. Instantaneous fuzes only will be used.

4. For the purposes of "S.O.S" T.M's will be controlled by Battalion Commanders. "S.O.S" Calls for T.M's will be sent by telephone to the Company H.Q's. nearest the emplacement, and transmitted thence to the emplacement by runner. The N.C.O. or man in charge of the detachment will report at Company H.Q's. when proceeding to the emplacement. An Infantry runner will be detailed to accompany the No.1 to the emplacement. This runner will then return to Company H.Q's. where he will be reserved for carrying "S.O.S" Calls to the detachment. The Call sent will be "S.O.S" and the name of the Sector.

5. The T.M.Battery Commander will inform Battalion Commanders and Artillery Liaison Officers at Battalion H.Q's. at 4 p.m. daily, as to what T.M's will be manned during the night.

6. In case of a raid being expected T.M. Battery Commander at H.34.b.00.97. will be warned so as to ensure T.M. support when required.

7. "S.O.S" Ammunition will be kept in damp-proof boxes, and will be turned over twice a week. After firing on "S.O.S" Lines the detachment will immediately prepare ammunition to replenish the "S.O.S" store.

8. RATE OF FIRE.
   6 rounds per minute for the first three minutes, then 4 rounds per minute for 7 minutes.

9. Further "S.O.S" targets will be issued according to progress in building emplacements.

LINES OF FIRE FOR "S.O.S" WILL BE AS FOLLOWS -

Location of T.M.	Sector.	Target.	To receive "S.O.S" Calls from:-	"S.O.S" calls to be transmitted through Coy.H.Q. at:-
N.10.a.15.70.	(S.O.S. "C" (S.O.S. "D" (S.O.S. "E"	N.10.c.38.41.) N.10.b.39.00.) N.11.a.40.68.)	O.C.Right Battalion.	N.10.c.30.40.
N.4.d.59.65.	(S.O.S. "D" (S.O.S. "E" (S.O.S. "F"	N.10.b.74.40.) N.11.a.59.84.) N.5.d.55.27.)	O.C. LEFT Battalion.	N.5.a.45.00.
N.5.b.95.27.	(S.O.S. "E" (S.O.S. "F" (S.O.S. "G"	N.5.d.25.21.) N.6.c.14.36.) N.6.d.08.67.)	-do-	N.6.a.60.85.
H.36.c.80.80.	(S.O.S "G" (S.O.S. "H"	N.6.b.40.00.) O.1.a.37.90.)	-do-	H.36.d.05.70.
H.36.d.27.63.	(S.O.S. "G" (S.O.S. "H"	N.6.b.80.40.) N.6.b.85.54.)	-do-	-do-
H.36.d.40.80.	(S.O.S. "F" (S.O.S. "G" (S.O.S. "H"	N.6.c.80.68.) N.6.b.50.16.) O.1.a.05.82.)	-do-	-do-

27.11.1917.

Captain R.F.A.
D.T.M.O., 38th.Division.

SECRET.

39th DIVISIONAL TRENCH MORTAR BATTERIES

"S.O.S." ORDERS. — CENTRE GROUP.

1. 6" NEWTON T.M's will be manned by night as far as possible, in order to strengthen the Artillery "S.O.S" Barrage, covering the posts in the front line.

2. EACH GUN will have a separate "S.O.S" target for each post. These targets are selected points in or near the enemy's wire. Instantaneous fuses only will be used.

3. For purposes of "S.O.S" T.M's will be controlled by the Company Commander nearest the Emplacement. The N.C.O., or man in charge of the detachment will report to the Company Commander when proceeding to the Emplacement. An Infantry runner will be sent with him to the Emplacement. This runner will then return to Company H.Q., where he will stand by to carry "S.O.S" Orders from the Company Commander to the N.C.O. in charge of the Gun. The Order sent will be "S.O.S", and the name of the post.

4. Lines of fire for "S.O.S" will be as follows:-

Position of Gun.	Name of Post	Location of Target.	"S.O.S" Orders to be sent from Company H.Q., all:-
I.16.b., 75.33.	(EILEEN, (CYNTHIA, (CISSIE,	I.16.b., 21.0. I.16.a., 40.60. I.22.a., 15.45.	I.9.d., 95.08. Left Company Front Company.
I.15.c., 90.70.	(CYNTHIA, (CISSIE, (CARRIE, (AILEEN,	I.22.a., 40.60. I.21.b., 75.40. I.21.b., 90.40. I.21.c., 85.55.	I.15.c., 85.42. (Centre Front Company.)
I.20.b., 65.22.	(CARRIE, (AUDREY, (ANNIE, (PAM,	I.21.b., 15.15. I.21.c., 72.68. I.21.c., 25.05. I.20.b., 85.85.	I.20.b., 85.80. (Right Front Company.)

5. RATE OF FIRE.
   6 Rounds per minute for first three minutes, then 4 rounds per minute for 7 minutes.

6. "S.O.S" ammunition will be kept in damp-proof boxes, and will be turned over twice a week. After firing on "S.O.S" lines, the detachment will immediately prepare ammunition to replenish the "S.O.S" store.

7. The T.M. Battery Commander will inform Battalion Commanders, and Artillery Liaison Officers at Battalion H.Q's, by 4-0 pm. daily as to what T.M's will be manned during the night.

8. In case of a raid being expected, T.M., Battery Commander at H.20.b., 58.77., will be warned so as to ensure T.M., support when required.

9. Further "S.O.S" targets will be issued according to progress in building Emplacements.

O.J.Fox

Captain R.F.A.,

21-11-17.

D.T.M.O., 39th Division.

SECRET.

38th. DIVISIONAL TRENCH MORTAR BATTERIES.

"S.O.S" Orders — Left Group.

1. 6" Newton T.M's will be manned by night as far as possible in order to strengthen the Artillery "S.O.S" Barrages.

2. Each gun will have a separate "S.O.S", target for each "Locality".   The targets are selected points in or near the enemy's wire.
Instantaneous fuzes only will be used.

3. For purposes of "S.O.S" fire, T.M's will be controlled by the Battalion Commanders. "S.O.S" Calls for T.M's will be sent by telephone to the Coy. H.Q's nearest the emplacement, and transmitted thence to the emplacement by runner. The N.C.O. or man in charge of a detachment will report at Coy.H.Q's when proceeding to the emplacement. An Infantry runner will be detailed at Coy.H.Q's to accompany the No.1 to the emplacement. This runner will then return to Coy. H.Q's, where he will be reserved for carrying "S.O.S" Calls to the detachment.
When an emplacement is near Battalion H.Q's a runner will be sent direct from Battalion H.Q's to the emplacement.
The call sent will be "S.O.S" and the name of the locality.

4. The T.M. Battery Commander will inform Battalion Commanders and Artillery Liaison Officers at Battalion H.Q's by 4 p.m. daily as to what T.M's will be manned during the night.

5. In case of a raid being expected, T.M.Battery Commander at C.28.a.70.50. will be warned, so as to ensure T.M. support when required.

6. "S.O.S" Ammunition will be kept in damp proof boxes, and will be turned over twice a week. After firing on "S.O.S" lines the detachment will immediately prepare ammunition to replenish the "S.O.S" store.

7. RATES OF FIRE:-

   6 rounds per minute for the first three minutes, then 4 rounds per minute for seven minutes.

8. Further "S.O.S" targets will be issued according to progress in building emplacements.

Please Acknowledge

O J Jones

Captain R.F.A.

21st. November 1917.   D.T.M.O., 38th.Division.

Copies to:-
"Z"/38th.T.M.B.
115th.Inf.Bde.
O.C.Left Sub-section 115 Inf.Bde.
O.C.Right   "   115 Inf.Bde.(3).
Left Group.
38th.Div. Arty.
File (2).

LINES OF FIRE FOR "S.O.S" WILL BE AS FOLLOWS:-

Position of T.M.	Number of Locality.	Location of Target.	To receive "S.O.S" calls from.	"S.O.S" Calls to be transmitted through Coy.H.Q.at
I.10.a.88.47 CENTRAL AVENUE.	(Locality 1. (Locality 2. (Locality 3. (Locality 4. (Locality 5.	I.17.a.15.75.) I.11.c.52.79.) I.11.a.32.30.) I.11.a.59.78.) I. 5.c.66.09.)	O.C. Right Sub-Section.	I.10.a.81.98. Right Front Coy.
I. 4.b.45.45 S.P.X.	(Locality 3. (Locality 4. (Locality 5. (Locality 6. (Locality 7.	I.11.a.55.61.) I.11.a.55.61.) I. 5.c.36.27.) I. 5.c.40.93.) I. 5.b.06.54.)	O.C. Right Sub-Section.	I.4.b.24.85. Left Support Coy.
C.28.d.60.30 WILLOW WALK.	(Locality 6. (Locality 7. (Locality 8 (Locality 9. (Locality 10. (Locality 11.	I. 5.b.10.28.) I. 5.b.11.99.) C.29.c.60.58.) C.29.a.42.27.) C.29.a.42.27.) C.29.a.75.95.)	O.C. Right Sub-Section.	I.4.b.24.85. Left Support Coy.
C.28.b.10.90 VANCOUVER.	(Locality 7. (Locality 8. (Locality 9. (Locality 10. (Locality 11. (Locality 12.	C.29.c.80.20.) C.29.c.43.73.) C.29.a.35.03.) C.29.a.42.40.) C.23.c.85.25.) C.23.c.75.60.)	O.C. Left Sub-Section.	Direct from Battalion H.Q's C.22.c.75.05.
C.22.d.05.60 SALONICA.	(Locality 10. (Locality 11. (Locality 12. (Locality 13. (Locality 14. (Locality 15.	C.29.a.68.58.) C.23.c.75.60.) C.23.a.70.05.) C.23.b.00.47.) C.17.c.85.36.) C.17.c.74.80.)	O.C. Left Sub-Section.	Direct from Battalion H.Q's C.22.c.75.05.

21st.November 1917.

Captain R.F.A.
D.T.M.O., 38th.Division.

WAR DIARY
or
INTELLIGENCE SUMMARY.

Army Form C. 2118.

December 1917.

38th Divisional T.M.B. War Diary.

WAR DIARY or INTELLIGENCE SUMMARY

Army Form C. 2118.

Place	Date	Hour	Summary of Events and Information	Remarks and references to Appendices
BIRDCAGE FM HQ C.4.6	1/12/17		Ommitted from War Diary of NOVEMBER. I.F.R. SHURFLUR detached from BASE on 29.11.17	
FRANCE July 36		2.0 – 3.0 pm	V/38 TMB fired 12 rounds 9.45" Target HOSTILE TM'S in INDEX AVENUE. Very high wind & shots [illegible]	
		2.0 – 2.40 pm	X/38 TMB fired 50 rounds 6" Target HOSTILE WIRE at I.31.d.55.55. Did a considerable amount of [illegible]	
		3.5 – 3.15 pm	Z/38 TMB fired 15 rounds 6" Target CENTAUR SUPPORT. Material shown up	
			I.F.R. SHURMER lectured on 6" TM course 15 at ARMY SCHOOL OF MORTARS	
	2/12/17	2.0 – 2.45 pm	Z/38 TMB fired 53 rounds 6" Target C.23.b.38.70 and I.5.c.87.27 Vent [illegible] at [illegible]	
	3/12/17	12 – 1.10 pm	Z/38 TMB fired 15 rounds 6" Target I.5.b.06.54. Registration of SOS line	
		1.45 – 2.0 pm	Y/38 TMB fired 23 rounds 6" Target DELANGRE FARM	All shots short
		1.0 – 2.0 pm	X/38 TMB fired 50 rounds 6" Target Wire at I.6.d.55.93.	Very promising
		1.0 – 2.0 pm	X/38 TMB fired 50 rounds 6" Target Wire at I.5.a.45.70. Was much [illegible] hundred by a [illegible]	
		2.20 – 2.50 pm	V/38 TMB fired 4 rounds 9.45" Target INCENSE AVENUE in a Telephone cable cut	Very disheartening
		1.50 – 2.45 pm	V/38 TMB fired 6 rounds 9.45" Target Delangre Farm. O/S change	
		1.10 – 2.45 pm	V/38 TMB fired 17 rounds 9.45" Target DELANGRE FARM.	
	4/12/17		Capt. O ST. JONES D.T.M.O. 38th Div. granted one months leave to U.K. Capt. W. Turk is acting D.T.M.O.	
		2.30 – 3.15	V/38 TMB fired 5 rounds 9.45" Registration [illegible] line. Expenditure limited owing to [illegible]	
		2.20 – 3.15	X/38 TMB fired 50 rounds 6" Target Wire at I.32.c.15.85	

WAR DIARY or INTELLIGENCE SUMMARY

Army Form C. 2118.

(Erase heading not required.)

Instructions regarding War Diaries and Intelligence Summaries are contained in F. S. Regs., Part II. and the Staff Manual respectively. Title pages will be prepared in manuscript.

Place	Date	Hour	Summary of Events and Information	Remarks and references to Appendices
BIRDCAGE FARM	4/12/17	2:15 - 3:0 pm	V/38 fired 12 rounds 9.45" Target MINNIE at C29 b 02.60. Shots hits on Target	
HQCA.6			V/38 fired 2 rounds 9.45" Target CENSUS Reserve BdVR rounds no short of target	
Essex Shaft 36		12.0 noon -1.0 pm	Z/38 fired 40 rounds 6" Target Support lines 15 dis 0834 INANG ABBEY	
	5/12/17	1:10 - 1:30 pm	X/38 fired 18 rounds 6" Target N6d 53.97 Good effect. Silenced enemy Cof Plantations	
		2:0 - 2:45 pm	V/38 fired 20 rounds 9.45" Target DE-ANGRE FARM. Ondirect hit on the FARM	
	6/12/17		2OR 903 16 LITTERS for unaccounted M/gunner Bud X/r8 TMB	
		10:30am -11:0am	V/38 fired 7 rounds 9.45" Target MINNIES in Dia. Very bad visibility	
		10:0 - 11:0 am	Z/38 fired 35 rounds 6" Target C29 c 60.53, C29 a 14.27, C29 d 14.69 Burst of fire	
	7/12/17	2:0 - 3:0 pm	V/38 fired 12 rounds 9.45" Target DE-ANGRE FARM. Good retaliation from trenches	
		1:10 - 2:15 pm	Z/38 fired 32 rounds 6" Target C29c 60.90, C29 a 04 27.27, I 15 b 10.25, I 15 b 11.44 C 29 d 15.49 Knocked SOS lines	
		6:10 - 8:25	V/38 fired 5 rounds 9.45" Target I 9.2.a 20.15 Regulation	
		5:0 - 5:5 pm	V/38 fired 3 rounds 9.45" Target INDEX Support & co-operation with pump artillery	
		5:0 - 5:5 pm	Y/38 fired 20 rounds 6" Target INDEX SUPPORT	
	8/12/17		2/NS Hunter Z/38 TMB attended leave to UK	
			Lt F.R. SHURMUR returns from week at "GREAT ARMY SCHOOL OF MORTARS"	

Army Form C. 2118.

WAR DIARY
or
INTELLIGENCE SUMMARY.
(Erase heading not required.)

Instructions regarding War Diaries and Intelligence Summaries are contained in F.S. Regs., Part II. and the Staff Manual respectively. Title pages will be prepared in manuscript.

Place	Date	Hour	Summary of Events and Information	Remarks and references to Appendices
BIRDCAGE FARM	8/12/17		12 ORs return from course at 1st Army School of Mortars	
HQ 46		1.5 – 1.45 pm	Y/38 TMB fired 15 rounds 9.45" Target Junction 71 Increase Supports In Enemy Avenue Blue/Red	
FRANCE 4/Bde		1.0 – 1.30 pm	Z/38 TMB fired 30 rounds 6" Target D.15.5.74 – 40.27 Shooting ? on target the target	
		12 NOON	Z/38 TMB fired 21 rounds 6" Target Censor Avenue. Robt T. Kino for Hostile TMs	
		1.0 – 1.20 pm	Z/38 TMB fired 54 rounds 6" Target 17.a.23.36 Good shot	
	9/12/17	11.0 am – 12 noon	V/38 TMB fired 10 rounds 9.45 Target Hostile TM in D.1.0.20 Duds fell on D.1.50.32	
		1.0 pm – 2.0 pm	Z/38 TMB fired 7 rounds 6" Target C.7.9.c.70.50	
		11.20 – 11.45	Z/38 TMB fired 4 rounds 6" Target Censor Drive	
			X/38 TMB fired 10 rounds 6" Target Cave at 13.13 40.65 Registration	
		2.30 – 3.15 pm	X/38 TMB fired 58 rounds 6" Target View of 4.b.d.20.82 Good effect	
	10/12/17	2.0 – 2.45 pm	Z/38 TMB fired 18 rounds 6" Target 17.8.05.10 Good effect. Several explosions caused. Rifle?	
			Casualty 2 ORs of 1/16 B.H.L.I. no casualties	
		11 am	Z/38 TMB fired 6 rounds 6" Target C.23.1.070 Retaliation Hostile TMs	
		2.5 – 3.10 pm	V/38 TMB fired 17 rounds 9.45" Target Wanderwegs C.23 d.1.0 Retaliation by our Day	
			V/38 TMB fired 3 rounds 9.45" Target TMs D.? Hostile TM observed	
		1.45 – 3.0 pm	X/38 TMB fired 52 rounds 6" Target Wire at 17.a.d.20.65	

A6945 Wt. W17422/M1160 350,000 12/16 D.D. & L. Forms/C/2118/14.

WAR DIARY
or
INTELLIGENCE SUMMARY.
(Erase heading not required.)

Army Form C. 2118.

Place	Date	Hour	Summary of Events and Information	Remarks and references to Appendices
BIRDCAGE FARM	11/2/17	2.10 – 2.55pm	Z/38 TMB fired 58 rounds 6" Target Wire V.16.570.05. Wire considerably thinned	
HQ 41.6		2.30 – 3.30pm	Z/38 TMB fired 51 rounds 6" Target C.29.c.70.50. Personnel returned	
Howe Shed 38		2.5 – 3.0pm	V/38 TMB fired 16 rounds 9.45" Target HQ 61 TM & Trench Junction O.22.a.15.75	
			New heavy Stokes gun wired Aquarium HE Position	
	12/2/17		1 NCO proceeds on Physical Training course to 1st Army Artillery School	
		11.30 – 12.15	Z/38 TMB fired 20 rounds 6" Target Wire 11a 70.99 – 66.90	
		2.25 – 3.30pm	V/38 TMB fired 14 rounds 9.45" against Incense Avenue 11.7a. New heavy pattern	
			1 OR reports from RAHQ 38th Division	
	13/2/17	12 – 12.10pm	X/38 TMB fired 20 rounds 6" Target Inchino Support V.11.B.85.70.60	
		12.0 – 1.0pm	Z/38 TMB fired 33 rounds 6" Target C.29.c.70.50 4" Minnie Trench location	
	14/2/17	1.50 – 3.30pm	V/38 TMB fired 3 rounds 9.45" Target Trench Junction C.29.a.10	
			6 rounds 9.45" Target Communication C.29.a.85.55	
			8 rounds 9.45" Target Minnie Trench C.29.a.02.65	
	15/2/17	11.30 – 11.50am	Z/38 TMB fired 3 rounds 6" Target Incandescent TR. Situation last	
		2.10 – 3.0pm	V/38 TMB fired 11 rounds 9.45" Targets (a) Minnie Trench Junction O.25.75	
			(b) Minnie O.16.60.30	

WAR DIARY
or
INTELLIGENCE SUMMARY.
(Erase heading not required.)

Army Form C. 2118.

Place	Date	Hour	Summary of Events and Information	Remarks and references to Appendices
BIRDCAGE Fm	15/1/17	1.0 — 2.30 p	X/38 TMB fired 100 rounds 6" Trgt 116 & 65.15. Nil unusual during period.	
NQ.CH.6	16/1/17		10 OR transferred from 38 KSO to TMBs & 42 MG Co. enemy Artillery	
Franvillebis			Capt. Brophy RGA & Corp. Burke attached to 38th Bn TMB in Field as for Army School of Mortars.	
		12.0 — 1.0 pm	Y/38 TMB had 3 rounds 9.45" Target Incline Support Battn. munitionn movement	
		12.0 — 1.0 pm	X/38 TMB had 40 rounds 6" Target incl. M.G. Support Rendezvous trench T?	
			GR 20 round of bombs on Belchasse. Sore casualties 2 OR wounded	
		2.30 — 3.15 pm	Z/38 TMB fired 50 rounds 6" Target C.29.c.70.50 Getting line on?	
17/1/17			Counter Battery Fell at Y/38 TMB Hendersonville to be ?	
			reconnaissance 11 Yeomen Lewis & Yeomen Richardson	
			3/E. Moore handed over Command GHP T MB and the cancelled	
		2.55 — 2.25 p	V/38 TMB fired 6 rounds 9.45" Target Conrad Support Sap	
			Rounds quite ? F continued to CENTAUR Row and	
			CENTAUR SUPPORT Road later on shown as ? Trench and	
		3.05 — 3.55 pm	Z/38 TMB had 5 rounds 6" Target 2nd 10.70.	
			One shell of Incandescent Trench wood and to a visibility	

WAR DIARY or INTELLIGENCE SUMMARY

Army Form C. 2118.

Place	Date	Hour	Summary of Events and Information	Remarks and references to Appendices
BIRDCAGE	18/2/17	2.5–3.0 pm	V/38 T.M.B. fired 11 rounds 9.45" Target H with T.M. O.16.c.30 no observations F.M.L.	
Fm H.9.c.b.		11.0– 11.2 noon	Z/38 T.M.B. fired 65 rounds 6" Target Blue and Trench C.20.d.40.20. Fire not effective	
Fosse 3/4/5/8	19/2/17	1.30– 2.30 pm	V/38 T.M.B. fired 10 rounds 9.45" Target Incense Support. 1st/H.55 I.17.a.60.30	
		12 noon– 1.45	X/38 T.M.B. fired 40 rounds 6" Target Blue abt S.16.d.9.20	
		12 noon– 1.30 pm	X/38 T.M.B. fired 60 rounds 6" Target Blue abt S.16.d.0.27	
		12.30– 12.50	X/38 T.M.B. fired 25 rounds 6" Target Blue I.31.d.9.56	
	20/2/17		X/38 T.M.B. shots observed in trench with 11/38 M.B. Observed hit 7	
			V/38 T.M.B. shot fire fired in accordance with 11/38 Rifle Order No.142	
			Z/38 T.M.B. fired 6 rounds 6" Target Hostile ... in Our Sandbag and ...	
			Other information recorded in ... Diary not held	
	21/2/17	11.30– 11.50 am	V/38 T.M.B. fired 5 rounds 9.45" Target ...	
	22/2/17		2/LT CH MOORE ... to ...	
		2.0– 3.0 pm	Y/38 T.M.B. fired 17 rounds 9.45" ...	
			Z/38 T.M.B. fired 20 rounds 6" ...	
		1.30– 2.10 pm	X/38 T.M.B. fired 49 rounds 6" ...	

Army Form C. 2118.

WAR DIARY
or
INTELLIGENCE SUMMARY.
(Erase heading not required.)

Instructions regarding War Diaries and Intelligence Summaries are contained in F. S. Regs., Part II. and the Staff Manual respectively. Title pages will be prepared in manuscript.

Place	Date	Hour	Summary of Events and Information	Remarks and references to Appendices
BIRDCAGE FARM	24/2/17	2.0–2.40	V/38 TMB fired 10 rounds gas Target Dohns House. Very successful.	
Hague			Z/38 TMB relieved in left section by 2nd Australian Division TMB	
Ferme 9lu(36.e.16)			X/38 TMB heard right & centre of line for 2 hours. Fired 25 rounds gas. TM (?) in (?) & others	
			Capt G.M. BROPHY and 1 NCO return to 1st Army's mess O.2 to 1st TA RB	
	25/2/17		1 NCO proceeds to 1st Army Artillery School (illegible) at Physical training	
			Lieut N.S HUNTER returns from leave to U.K.	
	27/2/17	10–2.0pm	X/38 TMB fired 50 rounds 6" Target Wet Indestrieds list enlarged	
			Lieut R.RANK posted to 38 Divisional TMB reporting this day	
			19 ORs (illegible) K 12/5H (illegible) N OR (illegible) in exchange a/b R & BW (illegible) 24/2/17	
	28/2/17		Lieut GG HARRIS and 1 DR Maitland K 6/22 R.W.F R.E.L joins Divisional TMB Hqrs	
	29/2/17	12.0 am–1.30	Y/38 TMB fired 47 rounds gas "Target W. 28 b 65	
		1.30–1.30	V/38 TMB fired 58 rounds gas "Target 9.1 min & 65 2nd & 21 T Magazine offices"	
		2.0–2.30	X/38 TMB fired 50 rounds 6" Target 3.1 c.6.10 = 13 d 20.30 (?) m	
			1 DR attached W. of BIRDCAGE FARM Hq–9.30	
	30/2/17	4.25–4.50	Y/38 TMB fired 46 rounds 6" Target Die A.D.30 and (illegible) 13.10.75.10	
			R.Welcher Bentley	

WAR DIARY
or
INTELLIGENCE SUMMARY.
(Erase heading not required.)

Army Form C. 2118.

Place	Date	Hour	Summary of Events and Information	Remarks and references to Appendices
BIRDCAGE FARM	30/7		COURT OF INQUIRY held at BIRDCAGE FARM H.Q. on case Sch/36/15 was witness Lt tc Lt	
HQ 46			death 19 Div A Hughes = DAC at B's TMB	
			1/35 TMB Kol Knowles. Truck Don 2 Waist N/W. vetelle	
Sh 28 GERMAN	31/7	2.15 – 4 pm	Situation of Front Armentes	
			1/35 TMB Left the west front the Division area	
			X/35 TMB held the left sects the Division MWA	
			Z/35 TMB relieve X/35 on W/36 a Gm	
			W/35 TMB cover the sects the Armenteires Front	
				Lt Col Fisher Lent a TMO at Someume

WAR DIARY
or
INTELLIGENCE SUMMARY.
(Erase heading not required.)

Army Form C. 2118.

JANUARY 1916

39th Divisional T.M.B. War Diary

WAR DIARY
or
INTELLIGENCE SUMMARY.
(Erase heading not required.)

Army Form C. 2118.

Place	Date	Hour	Summary of Events and Information	Remarks and references to Appendices
BIRDCAGE FM Hqrs G	1/8	2.0–3.0pm	X/38 TMB fired 50 rounds 6". Target Wire 012020.80 – 131675.0	
France/Belgium	1/8	2.0–3.0pm	X/38 TMB fired 40 rounds 6". Target Wire 012020.80 – 131675.10 good effect	
	2/8	12.20–12.50pm	V/38 TMB fired 10 rounds 9.45". Target MINNIES in O1.6. Slateworks Rd. Wytschaete	
			Very heavy 3rd saltpetre fire	
	3/8	1.0–1.30pm	Z/38 TMB fired 40 rounds 6". Target DERANGER 2xR 1t N10.6.90–80 Ploegsteert	
			M.G./CLARK RFA proceeds on leave to UNITED KINGDOM	
		2.15–3.0pm	X/38 TMB fired 40 rounds 6". Target Wire WARNEETON	
	4/8	2.15–2.30pm	X/38 TMB fired 20 rounds 6". Target Wire af 131650.55	
		2.25–3.20pm	V/38 TMB fired 20 rounds 9.45". Target DOLLS HOUSE N11C R16t 2x are fb	
		2.0–3.0pm	Z/38 TMB fired 17 rounds 6". Target DOLLS HOUSE af N11.a.50.70 Ploegsteert	
		3.0–3.30pm	X/38 TMB fired 40 rounds 6". Target Wire West of N6 d 10.60	
	5/8		LIEUT R. FRANKS RFA and 12 ORs proceeded to 16th Army TM School to course	
			NCOs + 30 men taken from 38th Div Signal School	
			CAPT O.S. JONES NC RFA BTY/O returned from leave to UK	
	6/8		LT. C.H. MOORE RFA returned from leave to UK	
	7/8	3.0–3.45pm	X/38 TMB fired 27 rounds 6". Target Wire in font of INDEX TR. Ploegsteert 011/2/75	

Army Form C. 2118.

WAR DIARY
or
INTELLIGENCE SUMMARY.
(Erase heading not required.)

Instructions regarding War Diaries and Intelligence Summaries are contained in F. S. Regs., Part II. and the Staff Manual respectively. Title pages will be prepared in manuscript.

Place	Date	Hour	Summary of Events and Information	Remarks and references to Appendices
BIRDCAGE HQ Coy 6	7/18		NCO returns from PT course at Ecole de Aultin School	
France Shaft 36	8/18	2.30- 3.30 pm	X/38 TMB fired 83 rounds 6" Target Q16 b/Q16 a/Q16 d/ Minenwerfer Tr	
	8/18		Lt H G POYNTER RFA transferred from X/38 TMB to command X/38 TMB	
			NCO proceeds to 38th Divisional Gas School	
	9/18	1.30- 2.10 pm	Z/38 TMB fired 40 rounds 6" Target Wire at O16 c 72.78 considerable damage	
		1.30- 2.10 pm	Z/38 TMB fired 40 rounds 6" Target Wire at T31 d 75.62	
	10/18	11.30- 12.30 pm	Z/38 TMB fired 30 rounds 6" Target O10 c 97.97 - O10 a 72.98 good results	
		11.30- 12.30 pm	Z/38 TMB fired 27 rounds 6" Target Inconsistent Tr Patrol reports enemy ready shelled Trench & Wire concrete dug out	
	11/18	2.45 pm	Y/38 T.M.B. fired 21 rounds 6" in retaliation for hostile Minenwerfer fire	
		3.20 pm	Y/38 T.M.B. fired 9 rounds 6" in retaliation for hostile Minenwerfer fire	
		2.15 pm	Z/38 T.M.B. fired 93 rounds 6" all hostile wire at O.I. a 59.87 I T.31 d 76.62. 30 yards gap made in wire at O.I. a 72.98.	
	12/18	9-5 am 3.00 pm	Y/38 T.M.B. fired 17 rounds 6" in retaliation for hostile Minenwerfer fire	
		2-0 pm	Y/38 T.M.B. fired 15 rounds 6" in registration of S.O.S. lines	
		3-0 pm		
	14/18	2.30 pm	Y/38 T.M.B. fired 5 rounds 6" in retaliation for hostile Minenwerfer fire	

Army Form C. 2118.

WAR DIARY
or
INTELLIGENCE SUMMARY.
(Erase heading not required.)

Instructions regarding War Diaries and Intelligence Summaries are contained in F. S. Regs., Part II. and the Staff Manual respectively. Title pages will be prepared in manuscript.

Place	Date	Hour	Summary of Events and Information	Remarks and references to Appendices
BIRDCAGE H.Q.C.H.6.	16/1/18	12 Noon	12TH DIVISIONAL T.M. BATTERIES took over the line from the 58TH DIVISIONAL T.M. BATTERIES and the latter proceeded to HAVERSKERQUE J.3a.C.8.T. for DIVISIONAL TRAINING	
HAVERSKERQUE	17/18		38TH T.M. B's commenced training including N.C.O's class for control of fire & map-reading, marching and rifle drill, gun drill, class for signallers, recreational training (tug of war, cross country running, rugby & association football) instruction in musketry, bayonet fighting, physical drill, saluting drill.	
T.3a.C.8.T.	19/18		LIEUT. R. RANK. R.G.A. and 12 O.R's from 6" T.M. course at 1st ARMY SCHOOL LIEUT. R.H. DEWHIRST R.F.A. and 6 O.R's proceeded to 1ST ARMY SCHOOL for 6" T.M. Course LIEUT. B.Y. CARR R.F.A. returned from leave U.K.	
	20/18		N.C.O. returned from DIVISIONAL GAS SCHOOL	
	28/18		LIEUT H.G. POYNTER R.F.A. returned from leave U.K. RANGE & EMPLACEMENTS for 6" T.M's completed for EXHIBITION & EXPERIMENTAL PURPOSES	
	31/1/18		N.C.O. proceeded on TURPINE COURSE at DIV. SCHOOL	

WAR DIARY
or
INTELLIGENCE SUMMARY.

(Erase heading not required.)

Army Form C. 2118.

Place	Date	Hour	Summary of Events and Information	Remarks and references to Appendices
38TH Division			SITUATION AT END OF MONTH.	
			38TH Division & T.M. Batteries engaged in Divisional Training.	

R.J. Summers Lieut
for J. Oakey Lt Col. R.F.A.
S.T.M.O. 38th Division.

Army Form C. 2118.

WAR DIARY
or
INTELLIGENCE SUMMARY.
(Erase heading not required.)

Vol 20

FEBRUARY 1918.

38TH DIVISIONAL T.M.B. WAR DIARY

Army Form C. 2118.

WAR DIARY
or
INTELLIGENCE SUMMARY.
(Erase heading not required.)

Instructions regarding War Diaries and Intelligence Summaries are contained in F. S. Regs., Part II. and the Staff Manual respectively. Title pages will be prepared in manuscript.

Place	Date	Hour	Summary of Events and Information	Remarks and references to Appendices
HAVERSKERQUE	1/3/18		38TH T.M.B's continued training including N.C.O's class for PATROL OF FIRE & MAP READING, MARCHING & RIFLE DRILL, GUN DRILL, GAS FOR SIGNALLERS, RECREATION TRAINING (TUG OF WAR, CROSS COUNTRY RUNNING, RUGBY & ASSOCIATION FOOTBALL) INSTRUCTION IN MUSKETRY, BAYONET FIGHTING SALUTING DRILL, PHYSICAL DRILL.	MAP REF'N SHEET 36 F
	2/2/18		LIEUT R.H. DEWHURST + 10 O.Rs return from ISTERTLY SCHOOL OF MORTARS. LIEUT. H.G. POINTER + 6 O.Rs ATTACHED TO 15TH ARMY SCHOOL OF MORTARS	
			LIEUT B.V. CLARK ADDED TO A BATTERY / 121 BRIGADE R.F.A.	
	3/2/18		LIEUT E.J. MILLER WILLIAMS proceeds to U.K on leave	
	6/2/18		L.G.R returned from tour of duty for course at M. School	
	9/2/18		Infantry attached for instruction of Musketry found as Sunshine	
			2/38 T.M.B disbanded and personnel of Medium T.M. Battery formed into 2 batteries X/38 & Y/38. Y/38 T.M.B. personnel sent to V/XI Corps H.T.M.B.	
			LIEUT. H.G. POINTER promoted CAPTAIN whilst in command of a MEDIUM T.M. BATTERY	

WAR DIARY or INTELLIGENCE SUMMARY

Army Form C. 2118.

Place	Date	Hour	Summary of Events and Information	Remarks and references to Appendices
INVERGEFFRE	11/3/18		Inspection instructor returned to his unit	
	12/3/18		4 officers attended Gas course at BASE	
	13/3/18		3 officers attended Camouflage course at BASE	
	14/3/18		Officer returned from Camouflage course	
			1 Officer & 3 O.R. attended demonstration of landing stages by Col. Burton	
ARQUINGHEM	17/3/18		4 O.R. treated on a Minor Engine Construction course at HOUDAIN	
			38th T.M.B's received 5 P.H. T.M.B's in ARMENTIÈRES HOUPLINES	SHEET 36
			& WEZ MACQUART SECTORS	N.W.
			1/38 T.M.B. fired 10 rounds "A" at nine in front of I.16.d.20.40. with good results	
H.me.2.3	18/3/18		LIEUT. J.N. COLLINS to H.Q.O.R. 1st Army. to 1st ARMY SCHOOL OF MILITARY ?	
	19/3/18		CAPT. H.G. POINTER & 8 O.R. return from 1st ARMY School of Mortars	
			LIEUT. F. J. MILLER. MILITAIRE returns from leave U.K.	
	20/3/18		2. O.R. return to Unit from MILITARY PRISON BASE.	
			1/38 T.M.B. fired 5 rounds "A" or C.29.C.50.30 in retaliation for ??	

WAR DIARY or INTELLIGENCE SUMMARY.

(Erase heading not required.)

Army Form C. 2118.

Instructions regarding War Diaries and Intelligence Summaries are contained in F. S. Regs., Part II. and the Staff Manual respectively. Title pages will be prepared in manuscript.

Place	Date	Hour	Summary of Events and Information	Remarks and references to Appendices
FRONNINGHEM			Hostile T.M.	
H.HG.33	22/2		Y/38 T.M. Battery fired 60 rounds 6" on line in front of INCIDENT	
			TRENCH with good result.	
			X/36 T.M.B. fired 5 rounds 2" in retaliation for hostile T.M.	
	23/2/18		Y/38 T.M.B. fired 95 rounds 6" at wire at INCH TRENCH I.16.d.50.95. to I.16.c.60.00. A gap made at I.16.d.53.98.	
	24/2/18		Y/38 T.M.B. fired 50 rounds 6" at INCH TRENCH & still wire cut. Further gap made.	
	25/2		X/36 T.M.B. fired 28 rounds 6" on S.O.S. lines and wire in CENSUS DRIVE in retaliation for hostile T.M.	
			Y/38 T.M.B. fired 50 rounds 6" at INCLEMENT TRENCH in wire cutting with good results	
	27/2/18		2/LIEUT. A. T. ASHBY R.F.A. posted to Y/38 T.M. BATTERY from BASE. 2/LIEUT. D.C. REES R.F.A. posted to X/38 T.M. BATTERY from BASE.	
	28/2/18		Y/38 T.M.B. fired 100 rounds 6" at hostile wire in front of	

WAR DIARY
or
INTELLIGENCE SUMMARY.

Army Form C. 2118.

(Erase heading not required.)

Place	Date	Hour	Summary of Events and Information	Remarks and references to Appendices
FRONT LINE	26/7/18		INCH TRENCH completely destroyed. X/38 T.M.B fired 25 rounds at C.27.C.60.85 in retaliation for hostile T.M. fire	
	27/7/18		X/38 T.M.B. fired 56 rounds at hostile wire in front of INCH TRENCH with good result	
	28/7/18		X/38 T.M.B. fired 22 rounds at hostile wire in front of INCH TRENCH. Battery of S.O.S. added	

Osborne Capt.
R.F.A.
D.T.M.O.
38th (WELSH) DIVISION

SECRET.

S.O.S. ORDERS   LEFT GROUP MEDIUM TRENCH MORTARS.

All previous S.O.S. Orders are cancelled. The following S.O.S. Orders will come into effect from today's date.

1. S.O.S. calls will be transmitted to the emplacements by two routes:-
   (a) From Battalion H.Q., (C.21.d.25.05.) by telephone to Trench Mortar Battery H.Q., (C.27.b.35.95.) thence by telephone to the emplacement.
   (b) In order to ensure that S.O.S. calls reach emplacements in spite of a possible breakdown of telephone communication, the following scheme of transmitting orders by runner from Company H.Q., will be carried out. The Nos 1 of each detachment will report every evening to the nearest Company Commander who will send a runner with him to find out the way to the emplacement. This runner will then return to Company H.Q. where he will stand by to carry S.O.S. calls to the gun. This method will not be used for the emplacement at C.28.d.60.30.

   The call sent will be S.O.S. and the name of the Sector attacked. These codes are the same as those used for Artillery S.O.S. fire.

2. The Trench Mortar Battery Commander at C.27.b.35.95. will inform the Battalion Commander and the Artillery Liaison Officer at Battalion H.Q. before 4-0 pm daily, as to which Trench Mortar emplacements will be manned during the night. The following emplacements will normally be manned:-

   LE RUAGE   C.18.c.65.10.
   WILLOW WALK   C.28.d.60.30.

3. In case of a raid being expected, The Trench Mortar Battery Commander will be warned as early as possible so as to ensure support from all Trench Mortars covering the threatened sector.

4. S.O.S. ammunition will be kept in damp-proof boxes and will be turned over once a week. After firing on S.O.S. lines the detachment will immediately procure and prepare 50 rounds to replenish the S.O.S. store.

5. Targets for S.O.S. will be as follows:-

Position and name of emplacement	S.O.S. call	Location of target	S.O.S. orders by runner to be transmitted from Coy. H.Q. at
WILLOW WALK C.28.d.60.30.	A	C.29.c.28.70.	
	B	C.29.d.96.15.	
	C	C.24.d.10.10.	
GHOST C.25.a.70.10.	A	C.29.c.76.97.	
	B	C.29.b.90.32.	C.28.a.60.20.
	C	C.24.d.10.21.	
SALONICA C.22.b.60.40.	B	C.29.a.57.49.	
	C	C.23.d.14.32.	C.22.a.65.25.
	D	C.24.d.54.70.	
LE RUAGE C.18.c.65.10.	D	C.24.b.X.45.	
	E	C.17.d.18.45.	C.24.a.65.25.
	F	C.17.a.50.51.	

   Rate of fire - 5 rounds per minute for the first 3 minutes.
                  then - 4 rounds per minute for 7 minutes.
   Instantaneous fuses only will be used.

6. Further S.O.S. targets will be issued according to progress in building emplacements.

                                                    O.V.
                                                    Captain R.F.A.
28-3-18.   Distribution:- Left Arty Group   B.T.M.O. 38th Division.
                          114 Inf Bde
                          13th Welsh Regt
                          14th Welsh Regt
                          15th Welsh Regt
                          X/38/TMB

SECRET.

S.O.S. ORDERS RIGHT GROUP MEDIUM TRENCH MORTARS.

1. For the purpose of S.O.S., as many Trench Mortars as possible will be brought into action every night in order to strengthen the Artillery S.O.S. barrages. Each gun will have a separate S.O.S. target for each S.O.S. sector within its zone. These targets are selected points in or near the enemy's front line wire, the general purpose of S.O.S. fire by Trench Mortars being to block the probable points of exit used by the hostile raiding parties.

2. S.O.S. calls will be transmitted to the emplacements by two routes :-

   (a) From Battalion H.Q., I.14.d.25.80., by telephone to Trench Mortar Battery H.Q., I.14.b.75.00., thence by telephone to the emplacement.
   (b) From the nearest Company H.Q. to the emplacements by runner. Nos 1 of each detachment will report every evening to the nearest Company Commander who will send a runner with him to find out the way to the emplacement. This runner will then return to the Company H.Q., where he will stand by to carry S.O.S. calls to the gun. This method of transmitting S.O.S. calls will only be used when there is a Company H.Q. within a short distance of an emplacement.

   The call sent will be S.O.S. and the name of the sector attacked. These sectors are the same as those used for Artillery S.O.S. fire.

3. The Trench Mortar Battery Commander will inform the Battalion Commander and the Artillery Liaison Officer at Battalion H.Q., at 4-0 pm daily, as to which Trench Mortar emplacements will be manned during the night.

4. In case of a raid being expected, the Trench Mortar Battery Commander concerned will be warned as early as possible so as to ensure support from all Trench Mortars covering the threatened sector.

5. S.O.S. ammunition will be kept in damp-proof boxes and will be turned over once a week. After firing on S.O.S. lines, the detachment will immediately procure and prepare 30 rounds to replenish the S.O.S. store.

6. Targets for S.O.S. will be as follows :-

Position and name of emplacement	S.O.S. call	Location of target	S.O.S. orders by runner to be transmitted from Coy H.Q. at
DEAD COW I.20.b.65.25.	Annie	I.21.c.40.10.	
	Audrie	I.21.b.10.10.	
	Carrie	I.21.b.40.25.	I.20.b.80.40.
	Cissie	I.21.b.40.25.	
	Clare	I.22.a.20.55.	
PARADISE ALLEY I.15.c.70.90.	Audrie	I.21.b.20.20.	
	Carrie	I.21.b.75.40.	
	Cissie	I.21.b.75.40.	I.15.b.65.50.
	Clare	I.22.a.42.72.	
	Cynthia	I.22.a.42.72.	
	Eileen	I.16.d.00.10.	
BRICK STREET I.15.b.75.55.	Cissie	I.22.a.20.55.	
	Clare	I.22.a.42.90.	
	Cynthia	I.22.a.42.90.	I.15.b.25.85.
	Eileen	I.16.d.15.95.	
	Evelyn	I.16.b.50.00.	
ENITH WALK I.16.a.30.70.	Clare	I.22.a.75.90.	
	Cynthia	I.22.a.75.90.	I.15.b.25.85.
	Eileen	I.16.c.95.70.	
	Evelyn	I.16.b.70.15.	

LOTHIAN   Evelyn   I.14.b.87.35.
I.10.c.85.80.
_____

   Rate of fire - 6 rounds per minute for the first 3 minutes
           then - 4 rounds per minute for 7 minutes.

   Instantaneous fuses only will be used.

7. Further S.O.S. targets will be issued according to progress in
   building emplacements.

                                          O J Jones

                                          Captain R.F.A.
   25-2-18.   D.T.M.O. 38th Division.

           Copies to -   X/38/Trench Mortar Battery.
                          Right Group, 38th Div. Arty.
                          115 Infantry Brigade (3)
                          38th Div. Arty.

SECRET

S.O.S. ORDERS   CENTRE GROUP MEDIUM TRENCH MORTARS.

1. For the purpose of S.O.S., as many Trench Mortars as possible will be brought into action every night in order to strengthen the Artillery S.O.S. barrages. Each gun will have a separate S.O.S. target for each S.O.S. sector within its zone. These targets are selected points in or near the enemy's front line wire, the general purpose of S.O.S. fire by Trench Mortars being to block the probable points of exit used by hostile raiding parties.

2. The Divisional front is covered by two Trench Mortar Batteries, the inter-battery boundary being the ARMENTIERES-LILLE Railway, the Centre Brigade is thus covered by portions of two Batteries. The forward H.Q. of the Left Trench Mortar Battery is at C.27.b.57.95., and the forward H.Q. of the Right Trench Mortar Battery is at I.14.b.75.00.
   S.O.S. orders will be transmitted to the emplacements by two routes:-
   (a) By telephone from Battalion H.Q., I.3.d.75.70., to Left Trench Mortar Battery (C.O.14) via C.O. 25. in case of an attack on the front North of the ARMENTIERES-LILLE railway, to Right Trench Mortar Battery H.H.12 via H.H.34 in case of an attack on the front South of the railway. *In case of an attack on S.O.S. Sector 'H' & K. both TM Batteries will be warned*
   (b) By runner from the nearest Company H.Q. to the emplacements. Nos 1 of each detachment will report to the nearest Company Commander every evening who will send a runner with him to find out the way to the emplacement. This runner will then return to the Company H.Q. where he will stand by to carry S.O.S. calls to the gun. This method of transmitting S.O.S. calls will only be used when there is a Company H.Q. within a short distance of an emplacement.

   The call sent will be S.O.S. and the name of the sector attacked. These sectors are the same as those used for Artillery S.O.S. fire.

3. The Trench Mortar Battery Commander will inform the Battalion Commander and the Artillery Liaison Officer at Battalion H.Q., at 4-0 pm daily as to which Trench Mortar emplacements will be manned during the night.

4. In case of a raid being expected, the Trench Mortar Battery Commander concerned will be warned as early as possible so as to ensure support from all Trench Mortars covering the threatened sector.

5. S.O.S. ammunition will be kept in damp-proof boxes and will be turned over once a week. After firing on S.O.S. lines the detachment will immediately procure and prepare 50 rounds to replenish the S.O.S. store.

6. Targets for S.O.S. will be as follows :-

Position and name of emplacement	S.O.S. call	Location of target.	S.O.S. orders by runner to be transmitted from Coy. H.Q. at
LOTHIAN I.10.c.85.30.	G H	I.11.c.32.42. I.11.a.35.30.	
PLANK AVENUE I.4.b.45.45.	H K L M N	I.11.a.35.30. I.5.c.85.28. I.5.c.25.62. I.5.b.10.50. I.5.b.08.56.	I.4.b.30.75.
COMPANY'S DELIGHT C.25.d.30.00.	K L M N	I.5.c.68.85 I.5.d.10.50. I.5.b.10.27. I.5.b.15.70.	I.4.b.30.75.
WILLOW WALK C.25.d.50.30.	N	C.29.d.15.00.	I.4.b.30.75.

Army Form C. 2118.

WAR DIARY
or
INTELLIGENCE SUMMARY.
(Erase heading not required.)

38TH DIV. T.M. BATTERIES
MARCH 1917

WAR DIARY or INTELLIGENCE SUMMARY

Army Form C. 2118.

(Erase heading not required.)

Place	Date	Hour	Summary of Events and Information	Remarks and references to Appendices
ERQUINGHEM H.14.c.3.3.	1918 MAR.1		Y/38 T.M.B. fired 40 rounds 6" mortar in front of INCH TRENCH with effective results	
			X/38 T.M.B. fired 32 rounds 6" wire cutting T.11.a.60.88 with good results	
			N.C.O. went to Infantry Bde at 6pm. Arrived	
	2		X/38 T.M.B. fired 67 rounds 6" as wire cut T.11.a.60.80 with good results	
	3		Y/38 T.M.B. fired 10 rounds 6" on instructions for shoot M.T.M. fire	
			Y/38 T.M.B. fired 65 rounds 6" in support of raid on hostile trenches by our Infantry	
			X/38 T.M.B. fired 18 rounds 6" in retaliation for hostile T.M. fire and 35 rounds 6" on wire at C.29.c.90.55 with good results	
			L.O.R sent to convoy of ammunition of Minor Dymples	
	4		X/38 T.M.B. fired 16 rounds 6" wire cut C.29.c.60.55 with fair results	
	5		Y/38 T.M.B. fired 92 rounds 6" at wire at I.11.a.62.75 during day	

WAR DIARY
or
INTELLIGENCE SUMMARY.
(Erase heading not required.)

Army Form C. 2118.

Place	Date	Hour	Summary of Events and Information	Remarks and references to Appendices
Ruyaulcourt H.4.c.33	MAR 5		Wire in front of trench.	
			1/38 T.M.B. fired 1 round 6" at C29c in retaliation for hostile T.M. fire. N.C.O. & 3 O.R.s returned from School of Instruction from leave.	
	6		1/38 T.M.B. fired 15 rounds 6" at hostile wire at T.11.a.6.55 with good results & 8 rounds 6" at C.29.c in retaliation for hostile T.M. fire	
			Lt. E.T. MILLER W.W. A.M.C. posted to B/121 Bde. R.F.A. Lt M.O.C. Capt H.G. POYNTER proceeded on leave in leave [Louis Boulard]	
	7		Lt. J.N. COLLINS & 10 O.R.s returned from 1st Army school of Musketry. 1/38 T.M. Battery fired 15 rounds late wire in front of Central Trench with good results	
	8		1/38 T.M.B. fired 19 rounds 6" wire cutting in front of INCH DESCENTE and 18 rounds in retaliation for hostile T.M. fire	
	9		1/38 T.M.B. fired 21 rounds 16" wire cutting in front of WEALDES CENT TRENCH & 17 rounds retaliation for T.M. fire	

WAR DIARY
INTELLIGENCE SUMMARY.
(Erase heading not required.)

Army Form C. 2118.

Place	Date	Hour	Summary of Events and Information	Remarks and references to Appendices
ERQUINGHEM H4.C.3.3.	MAR 10th		X/38 T.M.B. fired 60 rounds 6" were cutting at CENTAUR TR.	
			Y/38 T.M.B. fired 38 rounds 6" on S.O.S. lines	
	11th		X/38 T.M.B. fired 12 rounds on "unbroken" S.O.S. lines & 6 rounds were cutting CENTAUR TR. & 8 rounds retaliation on hostile T.M. fire	
			Y/38 T.C.B. fired 30 rounds 6" & 6" were cutting INCANDESCENT TR.	
	12th		2/Lt A.G.N. CARSWELL fired Y/38 T.M.B. from BATS	
			X/38 T.M.B. fired 30 rounds 6" in support of raid by our 3rd contingent on hostile trenches.	
			Y/38 T.M.B. Battery fired 30 rounds 2" were cutting INCANDESCENT TR. & 3 rounds on S.O.S. lines	
			Y/38 T.M.B. fired 40 rounds 6" on S.O.S. lines	
			Hors. G. return. Wagon. struck by hostile shell. Killing Driver Binks & two mules, wounding Dvr Divine -	
	13th		Y/38 T.M. Battery fired 70 rounds 6" were cutting INCANDESCENT TR. HS normal. Retaliation	
	14th		D.T.M.O. attended Divnl Conference of D.T.M.O.s of Divisions	

WAR DIARY
or
INTELLIGENCE SUMMARY.
(Erase heading not required.)

Army Form C. 2118.

Place	Date	Hour	Summary of Events and Information	Remarks and references to Appendices
ERQUINGHEM H.4.c.33	Mar. 26		1 O.R. returned from CORPS SIGNAL SCHOOL.	
	27		Y/38 T.M.B. fired 34 rounds 6" in registration of target.	
	28		Y/38 T.M.B. fired 128 rounds in support of Raid on hostile trenches by S.W.B.	
			X/38 T.M. Battery fired 11 rounds 6" in registration of target.	
	29		Capt. W.A. Fox & Lt. S.V. Collins returned from U.K. leave	
	30		X/38 T.M. B. fired 42 rounds in co-operation of Raid on hostile trenches by our Infantry	

Owen
Capt. R.F.A.
D.T.M.O. 38th DIV.

WAR DIARY or INTELLIGENCE SUMMARY

Army Form C. 2118.

Place	Date	Hour	Summary of Events and Information	Remarks and references to Appendices
ETAING[?]HEM H.Q.3.			1ST ARMY.	
	MAR 14		Y/38 T.M. Battery fired 24 rounds 6" wire cutting at T.11.a.5.1.50.	
			X/38 T.M. Battery fired 30 rounds 6" in registration & wire cutting T.S.C. 69.07.	
	15		Y/38 T.M.B. fired 24 rounds 6" wire cutting & harassment support trench in conjunction with an aeroplane. 15 rounds registration of targets.	
			X/38 T.M.B. fired 65 rounds wire cutting & registration at T.15.b. & c.	
	17		Y/38 T.M.B. fired 18 rounds retaliation for hostile T.M. fire.	
	19		2/Lt T.F. Berger wounded G.S.W. left calf & admitted to Hospital.	
	24		X/38 T.M.B. fired 5 rounds 6" C.03.d.05.10. retaliation.	
	21-22		2/Lt R.M.R & 2/Lt G.N. CARSWELL admitted to Hospital suffering from flu. Several officers with the personnel of 2 sections of Y/38 T.M. Battery.	

V. Corps.
Third Army.

WAR DIARY

38th DIVISIONAL TRENCH MORTAR BATTERIES.

A P R I L

1 9 1 8

WAR DIARY

7TH DIVISIONAL TRENCH MORTAR BATTERIES.

APRIL 1918.

Date	Place	Time	
1st	Erquinghem		X/38 T.M.B. fired 12 rounds in retaliation for hostile T.M. fire in HOUPLINES Section.
2nd	"		Y/38 " " 20 " " S.O.S. lines in ARMENTIERES sector.
3rd	"		Y/38 " " 6 " in registration.
4th	"		X/38 " " 24 " " retaliation for hostile T.M. fire in HOUPLINES sector.
5th	"		Y/38 " " 6 " " " " " " " - ARMENTIERES "
			10.9.20.R. } X/34 } arrived as advance party of 34th Div. T.M. Bo.
			4. " } Y/34 }
7th	"		Heavy bombardment of ARMENTIERES with gas shells during the night. Lieuts J.V. Collin, Y/38, evacuated from heavy Remainder of personnel of 34th T.M.Bo. arrived in ERQUINGHEM prior to taking over
8th	"		4 O.R. a/m despite gassing. Night 8/9th 34th T.M.B. relieved in forward area by 34th T.M.B.
9th	"	6 a.m. 10 a.m.	Advance party of 38th T.M.B. proceeded to HAVERSKERQUE to take over billets. Rly. completely blocked, cancelled owing to hostile attack in our sector. D.T.M.O's H.Q. in ERQUINGHEM evacuated owing to hostile shell fire. is later shown, destroyed by fire. All records of unit, together with officers' kit + unit in accordance with orders from R.A.H.Q. Batteries withdrawn W of Lys, bringing with them 12 original T.M. pieces from STEENWERCK, under orders from R.A.H.Q. Batteries marched to STEENWERCK under orders from R.A.H.Q. and were attached to 34th D.A.C. Captain O'Jones, H.G., R.F.A., D.T.M.O. attached to R.A.H.Q. " Lieut. For R.W. Red. Regt., o/c Y/38 T.M.B. appointed acting D.T.M.O. " H.G. Poyntes, R.F.A., o/c X/38 T.M.B., admitted hospital gassed

WAR DIARY
7TH DIVISIONAL TRENCH MORTAR BATTERIES

DATE	PLACE	TIME	
10th	STEENWERK	5:30am	Advance orders from 34th D.A.C., Batteries marched to BLANCHE MAISON, & later to OUTTERSTEENE. No transport being available, 6 pairs went dumped at Reinforcement Camp STEENWERK.
11th	OUTTERSTEENE		X/38 T.M.B., moves hist. Lt. O.A. Frey R.F.A., Wounded for work on Ammunition Dump W.J. Bartlett. Y/38 T.M.B. attached to No.2 Section 34th D.A.C. BT.M.O. & H.Q. remainder att.d to H.Q., 34th D.A.C. H.Q. & Y/38 marched own own from 34th D.A.C. to LE SOUVERAIN. E.g. HAZEBROUCK. 1 O.R. missing, cause unknown.
12th	LE SOUVERAIN		Lieut J.V. Golden R.F.A. & 1 O.R. attd RAHQ. 34th D.A.C. moved at short notice to ST MARIE - KAPPEL. No transport being available, H.Q. & Y/38 T.M.B. were unable to follow till next day, and remaining 6 pairs hrs to be marched.
13th	GODEWAERSVELDE		H.Q. & Y/38 T.M.B. rejoined 34th D.A.C. at GODEWAERSVELDE X/38 moved Dump to ST SANS KAPPEL.
14th	"		Both batteries placed under orders of DT.M.O. for work on Ammn. Dump. Y/38 T.M.B. relieved X/38 T.M.B.
15th	"		1 O.R. & 20 O.R. X/38 T.M.B. reported at WIPPENHOEK to form Rear Demb
18th	"		
19th	"		17 signallers attached to R.A. signal section B.O.R. att.d R.A.H.Q.

WAR DIARY
8TH DIVISIONAL TRENCH MORTAR BATTERIES

Date	Place	Time	
20th	RODENWAPSVELDE		Dump moved from ST JANS KAPPEL to HT. KOKEREELE MMY ROENTEV
21st	"		Remainder of X/38 proceeded to new dump for duty
22d	"		To R. & M.S. from 38/D.A.C. posted to 122 B.Bgy. R.F.A.
23d	"		Lieut. F.R.Shewring R.F.A. "A"/Lieut. A.J.Dalby R.F.A. & 26 O.R. proceeded to below to bring back ammunitions.
24th	"		16 signallers rejoined from R.A. signal section
25th	L10(Sh.t 27)		Batteries with 84/D.A.C. moved by road to rejoin L10(Sh.t 27)
26th		20.90 O.R. returned to WIPENHOEK dump for duty
			16 signallers attached R.D. Sig. section
			Lieut. Shewring, Lieut. Ashby, & 2.O.R. rejoined from Remount Duty
28th			Batteries moved to rejoin L7d (Sh.t 27)
			Lieut. A.N.G. Benwell (R.F.A.) rejoined from Hospital to T/38 T.M.B.
			2 O.R. remainder
29th			Lieut. R.H.Moore R.F.A. & 10 O.R. attached for duty to 121 Bde R.F.A.
			" A.J. Ashby R.F.A.
			" D.C.Rea R.F.A.} & 10 O.R. attached to T " 122 "
			" A.N.G. Benwell (R.F.A)

1/5/18.
Slitten Kingham
Ap.Cmo. 38th Divn

(2)

GHOST   M   C.29.c.80.20.
C.28.a.70.10.

    Rate of fire - 6 rounds per minute for the first 3 minutes
              then - 4 rounds per minute for 7 minutes.

    Instantaneous fuzes only will be used.

7.   Further S.O.S. targets will be issued according to progress in
    building emplacements.

O.J. Jones

                                            Captain R.F.A.
25-2-16.   D.T.M.O. 38th Division.

    Ø   Not yet completed.

       Copies to -   X/38/Trench Mortar Battery
                          Y/38/Trench Mortar Battery
                          Centre Group, 38th Div. Arty.
                          113 Infantry Brigade (2)
                          38th Div. Arty

Army Form C. 2118.

WAR DIARY
or
INTELLIGENCE SUMMARY.
(Erase heading not required.)

Instructions regarding War Diaries and Intelligence Summaries are contained in F.S. Regs, Part II. and the Staff Manual respectively. Title pages will be prepared in manuscript.

T.M.B⁴⁵
Y.T.M.B⁴⁵
Vol 23

Place	Date	Hour	Summary of Events and Information	Remarks and references to Appendices
ST JANTER BIEZEN.	1918. May 2.		1.O.R. wounded in action.	
	7.		2.O.R. injured in action.	
	8.		Captain J.W. Foy. M.C. appointed D.T.M.O. 36th Division 4/5 38th Div 90th I.O.R.	
	11.		Captain V.C. Ryall R.H.A. posted to Y/38 T.M. Bty from 55th D.T.C.	
	10.		2/Lt J Oxley posted to X Bty from 55th D.T.C.	
	11.		All personnel & X/Y Bty's wounded from ammunition dumps.	
	12.		X & Y Bty marched to PROVEN.	
	19.		X Bty marched to HOBEZINE Y Bty marched to WATTENBECK where they entrained.	
REZINGHEM	20.		X Bty detrained at DOURLENS & Y Bty at AMIENS both Batteries marched to BILLETS at GEZAINCOURT.	
	20.		Capt D.Simmons & Lieut J.W.Collins returned from 1st A.P.M.	
	21.		2/Lieut C.H.Neale returned from 191 Bgde R.F.A.	
	28.		2/Lieut D.C. Rees Y Bty transferred to Y/191 Bde from 122 Bgde R.F.A. 2/Lieut W.S. Huntley posted to Y Bty ... 15th ...	
	29.		2/Lieut A.O. d'U.A. Hibbard posted to X Bty from 30th D.T.C.	
RAINNE CHEVAL	31.		X & Y Bty's marched to RAINNE CHEVAL.	

6. Toner
Capt R.F.A
D.T.M.O. 38th (WELSH) Div.

Army Form C. 2118.

WAR DIARY
or
~~INTELLIGENCE SUMMARY~~
(Erase heading not required.)

Vol 24 SECRET

38TH (WELSH) DIVISIONAL TRENCH MORTAR BATTERIES

JUNE 1918.

Army Form C. 2118.
Sheet 7

WAR DIARY
or
INTELLIGENCE SUMMARY.
(Erase heading not required.)

Instructions regarding War Diaries and Intelligence Summaries are contained in F. S. Regs., Part II. and the Staff Manual respectively. Title pages will be prepared in manuscript.

Place	Date	Hour	Summary of Events and Information	Remarks and references to Appendices
GEZAINCOURT RAINCHEVAL	1/6/15 June		The batteries marched from GEZAINCOURT (LENS 11 MAP) to RAINCHEVAL where they bivouacked in the Curing in N.18.c. (sr MAP. FRANCE 57D) the rest of that day, and the 3 days which followed were spent in the completion of reorganization in new units, this consisting of hew and experienced officers and N.C.O.s deputated to relieve the front on which the batteries there about to relieve the 63rd (Naval) M.T.M.B	
	4/6/15			
	4/6/15			
VARENNES	5/6/15	3pm	On this date the batteries marched to VARENNES near HQ. were established at P25d.3.4. and relieved the 63rd (Naval) Div. M.T.M.B. The relief was completed by this time. 70.1 section of Y/38 and Y/38 that taken over from X/63 and Y/63 in the forward offensive positions of those batteries, and 70.2 section of Y/38 in four batteries had similarly relieved X/63 and Y/63 in their reserve or defensive positions used by the latter. The 30 M.T.Ms. remained at the HQ. in VARENNES where they thoroughly cleaned, and organised as new billets.	Appendix I
	6/6/15	2.30pm to 4.35pm	During these tours the guns in the forward positions fired 134 rounds. More than half of this were expended upon reparation of S.O.S. lines. Some batteries and some newly laid out are on the outgoing batteries. The remainder were expended mainly for the further defence of the line T.M. fire, but a few upon targets indicated in retaliation for hostile T.M. fire, but a few upon targets indicated by the enemy in bad retrieval	

Army Form C. 2118.

Sheet 2

WAR DIARY
or
INTELLIGENCE SUMMARY.
(Erase heading not required.)

Place	Date	Hour	Summary of Events and Information	Remarks and references to Appendices
Mesnil	7/9/18	12.45pm to 11.9pm	During this period the guns fired 140 rounds. The bulk of the ammunition was expended upon new enemy works and suspected hostile T.M. emplacements, but the remainder was discharged at all times in retaliation for a hostile bombardment.	
	8/9/18	10.30pm to 11.35pm	274 rounds were fired from our howitzers. J.M. emplacements received a great part of this attention, also enemy posts. 133 rounds however were fired at the T.M. comforters to the N. of assembled. The artillery carried out harassing fire upon known enemy lines on our left division front.	
	9/9/18		During the air day on a limited rounds were expended up to the enemy works, and [?] the air SOS lines of the guns. The [?] weight [?] the section [?] received fire in answer [?] from the [?] trenches and [?] company firing [?] [?] [?] targets and SOS lines.	
	10/9/18	10pm to 8pm	Emplacements and [?] [?] [?] [?] rounds. was continued, at the cost of 218 rounds. 9 rounds T.M. fire was received by [?] the day. Retaliation for hostile T.M. fire accounted for expenditure of 70 rounds, and enemy works for the rest.	
	11/9/18 1.30pm to 6.15pm			
	12/9/18 10.5am to 1.30pm		The normal course of weapons firing on this sect, resulted a total of 132 rounds, thirty in a direct hit upon a hostile trench stock, which was promptly followed up by six rounds gun fire.	

Army Form C. 2118.
Sheet 3

WAR DIARY
or
INTELLIGENCE SUMMARY.
(Erase heading not required.)

Place	Date	Hour	Summary of Events and Information	Remarks and references to Appendices
MESNIL	13/6/18		[illegible handwritten entries]	M.P.
	19/6/18	2.30 – 4.15pm		
	19/6/18			
	20/6/18	2.45pm – 4.49pm		
	20/6/18	2pm – 3.20pm		
	20/6/18	10am – 11am		
	20/6/18	3am		
	20/6/18	12 mid – 6.30am		Secret Questions

Army Form C. 2118.

Sheet 4

WAR DIARY
or
INTELLIGENCE SUMMARY.

(Erase heading not required.)

Place	Date	Hour	Summary of Events and Information	Remarks and references to Appendices
MESNIL	21/6/18		a raid by 113th & 115th Infantry Brigade on the enemys emplacements & trenches extending on the line 2.35.b.55,50 to Q.23.a.55,00. (Ref: WM France 57 D SE.) The targets assigned to Brohs. were: in Bray, the N. edge of ANELAY WOOD and the enemy trenches and dugouts along & N. of the railway on Q.4 M.a & c.Q.35.b v.c	Appendix 31
	20.6.18	12mn-3.35am	On 20.6.18 the Bde. Artillery Zero = Z=0 Z=R84 2nd 50 mins 1/35 MW & fired 452 rounds on the a 2.35 b.i.c. in turn to 2.35.d. harassing relatively was in he most fully limited and the guns 9/78 Bde's guns firing every 10 minute and the enemy guns or dug outs. This heavy arty fire 14 and the cont[in]gent arty M.G. of M.G. and caused the battery no cas Bde fire their 2 & lost dets. arty M.G. STIM3H & no 3033 rounds on the bus fire their silence, also got on 2.35.b.i.c	
	21.6.18	2.25am-6.7.35am	4/05 fired in support of the tech well attack of 235 rounds were fired on the range C=0dcs(Km2334) Gx 126c 7,326c.c	
		30-3.35am	610 rounds were fired out C.S.Ireon with the 19/10th Kings Regts Experience the enemy further weakening the extension to avenge the assembly of his vast in this ammo for further assistance to the cost of our food and 7th to dig more trenches in this sector. Equipment L of our pivot and interest. & hampering and 3 L of our vans groups bring out of action	
	23.6.18		the enemy & activity of the Cossiers was more minimal with our again noted clearly shown in places	

Army Form C. 2118.
Sheet 5

WAR DIARY
or
INTELLIGENCE SUMMARY.
(Erase heading not required.)

Instructions regarding War Diaries and Intelligence Summaries are contained in F. S. Regs., Part II. and the Staff Manual respectively. Title pages will be prepared in manuscript.

Place	Date	Hour	Summary of Events and Information	Remarks and references to Appendices
HEDIM	21.6.15	7pm – 6pm	87 Rounds Expended	
	22.6.15	3pm – 4.30pm	25 Rounds Expended	
			108 Rounds by 4/38 in bombardment of village	Relative ease and dearness of ammunition expenditure was too
	22.6.15	3pm – 4.45pm	110 Rounds Expended	directed against enemy works
	23.6.15	9.30am – 6.30pm	118 Rounds Expended	MG's 2 nine, MH, 223 G 16,25
	24.6.15	6.11 AM		LG 29.3/15
		6.4.20 pm	120 " "	Irma Edge
	25.6.15	4pm to 6.30pm	52 (4/38 selected against ? Karoly)	water 4/38 of enemy
	26.6.15	11.45pm – 6.15pm	43 Rounds Expended	Engineer 4/15
			The fire of the 26" commenced early. he went to intensive a flexical opening of the cutting opened along the whole front when fire for near to vicinity the enemy and district. Upon attempting preliminary operations to the T.P. this Art. This on the 25/6.15 and 29 to a light howen parallel some hundred in all, was so intended (in addition to the sanctuary the usual several of enemy movements and violation of lights MG. fire, attack, alternative agreed action, and violation of lights MG. fire, shell of reg. 7.m. extreme 6 after was comprised to 21.6.15 upon two such sites were 7.M extreme(?)	
Fort R	24.6.15		This destruction fire was especially warmer with afternoon of of	
	27.6.15		this date 154 rounds being used upon that what was must elsewhere	
	28.6.15		also a quiet wind and the knowledge of elevating and finding	
	29.6.15		already referred to. We were in of fire the strands on the tell to govern fit no safe unit the encampments lay. Some supposes and efforts	
			by several my destruction died of to upon the enemy front line were upon much damaged and very to	

Army Form C. 2118.

Sheet

WAR DIARY
or
INTELLIGENCE SUMMARY.
(Erase heading not required.)

Instructions regarding War Diaries and Intelligence Summaries are contained in F. S. Regs., Part II. and the Staff Manual respectively. Title pages will be prepared in manuscript.

Place	Date	Hour	Summary of Events and Information	Remarks and references to Appendices
			General. During the whole period under review the emplacements and dug-outs both of forward and reserve positions have been gradually improved and strengthened. In some cases fifty fascines have again improved and strengthened. The dug outs have been relined to secure the whole strength of the dug-outs. The emplacements are being systematically remodelled throughout. Great care has had to be exercised in the disposal of spoil, the enemy being extremely alert. In spite of continual and endeavour damage to wire by the enemy's continual shelling, the system of emplacements temporarily communication. In spite of continual and endeavour damage to wire by the enemy's continual shelling, the system of emplacements temporarily communication. The days of emplacements temporarily supplies and maintenance to the Our tasks arranged. Malgré souvent, remnants supply arrangements for the enemy having to be carried through up from and various shellings for many consecutive hours all drinking water has had to be supplied in petrol tins by pony and the supply of rum, petrol oil etc. had to be effected in this time morning. If any degree of rapidity was to be ensured the casualties sustained had been surprisingly light.	

Army Form C. 2118.

WAR DIARY
or
INTELLIGENCE SUMMARY.
(Erase heading not required.)

APPENDIX I

Place	Date	Hour	Summary of Events and Information	Remarks and references to Appendices
Reference Map Sheet Fricourt 57d S.E.				

Location Post
X/38 I.M.B.

H.Q.   Q.28.a.95.65.

Emplacements   Q.28.b.51.23 ⎫
               Q.22.a.28.20 ⎬ Offensive
               Q.22.d.20.12 ⎭

               Q.27.a.06.86 ⎫
               Q.21.a.39.10 ⎬ Defensive
               Q.27.a.39.20 ⎭

Y/38 I.M.B.

H.Q.   Q.28.a.30.10

Emplacements   Q.34.b.10.84. ⎫
               Q.34.a.98.56. ⎪
               Q.34.b.05.25   ⎪
               Q.34.b.21.80   ⎪
               Q.34.b.30.84   ⎬ Offensive
               Q.34.b.30.91   ⎪
               Q.34.b.20.93   ⎪
               Q.34.c.46.8x   ⎪
               Q.34.c.60.92. ⎭

               Q.32.b.40.69 ⎫
               Q.32.b.90.77 ⎬ Defensive
               Q.27.a.15.60   ⎪
               Q.32.b.94.81. ⎭

Army Form C. 2118.

WAR DIARY
or
INTELLIGENCE SUMMARY.
(Erase heading not required.)

Instructions regarding War Diaries and Intelligence Summaries are contained in F. S. Regs., Part II. and the Staff Manual respectively. Title pages will be prepared in manuscript.

APPENDIX II

Place	Date	Hour	Summary of Events and Information	Remarks and references to Appendices
			Casualties	
	4-6-18		9 Reinforcements reports for duty	
	5-6-18		1 O.R. wounded in action, admitted to hospital	
	8-6-18		2 O.R. do do	
	9-6-18		1 O.R. killed in action. 3 O.R. wounded in action, admitted to hospital	
	10-6-18		Capt. O. Sheard M.C O.R. 10770 Admitted to hospital Sick	
	11-6-18		2/Lt A. Shield P.P.9 x/88/7MB do do.	
			1 O.R. to hospital	
	12-6-18		2 O.R. to hospital	
	12-6-18		3 Reinforcements reports for duty	
	13-6-18		1 O.R. to hospital	
	16-6-18		2/Lt G Hind O.R.A Back from D.A.C.	
			2/Lt J Gillies P.P.9	
			2/Lt J.S. Roberts P.P.9	
			1 O.R. to hospital	
	19-6-18		1 Reinforcement reports for duty	
			1 O.R. Hospital	
	23-6-18		1 O.R. Hospital	
	26-6-18		Reinforcement reports for duty	

Army Form C. 2118.

WAR DIARY
or
INTELLIGENCE SUMMARY.
(Erase heading not required.)

WAR DIARY JULY 1918

38th Divisional Train M.T. Section

Army Form C. 2118.

WAR DIARY
INTELLIGENCE SUMMARY
(Erase heading not required.)

Instructions regarding War Diaries and Intelligence Summaries are contained in F.S. Regs., Part II. and the Staff Manual respectively. Title pages will be prepared in manuscript.

Place	Date	Hour	Summary of Events and Information	Remarks and references to Appendices
VARENNES	1.7.18		Ref Map Franc Sheet 57a.	
			The month opened with two sections of each battery in the line, and one in Rest Billets at VARENNES, according to the usual routine. The latter were engaged in instructional parades of Lewis Gun, Musketry, Gas drill and Saluting Drill, and in the further improvement of the billets. Thus, coupled with numbers always required was made with the protection of the mens quarters and the long times from bomb-sid other splinters, and with a view to avoiding infection by the widely prevalent Influenza, who quarters were sanitized and the men little restricted.	
MESNIL	1.7.18	9.30 pm to 10 pm	The first events hour began with 82 rounds S.O.S. in the evening of July 1, at the request of the infantry holding the line, and attempts to reduce by bombardment this and two adjacent hostile strong points. This fell was answered with two minutes rapid fire by 3 hostile enemy bands. 3 S.O.S. lines were registered apart and during Fumble hostile minelays.	
	3.7.18 3:45pm to 4:45pm		attentive gun to 2 hostile TM's, 25 rounds being expended. Further hostile movays and a machine gun were engaged on the 4th and next day enemy works and an enemy trench were also bombarded. On the 6 th a prominent spot on the hostile lines was registered. The fated road in Q 23, d 30, a locality which strongly fell of any Red been observed in the preceding month.	
	4.7.18 5.7.18 6.7.18		During the first days of the month the enemy's trenches were temporarily quiet, although the harassing fire of other quarters of our own ensued machine battery firing, and developed on the 3, into a destruction along and comptines heavy, and of the trying hours was carried on b/5 battery's Forward R.O.P.S, although no evidence of damage or of that occasion. On one occasion the trolley lines was were shelled, and two "MENTOR" ammunition laden trains. A temporary shortage of 16" MENTOR ammunition later in the week, however, a further 600 rounds became available.	

WAR DIARY / INTELLIGENCE SUMMARY

Army Form C. 2118.

Place: MESNIL

When not firing, my detachments were engaged in digging their guns and the ground about their position, and in improving their emplacements by revetting and deepening the trenches. The employment of my entire garrison was also required. But once my sole extra material could not meet my requirements. The emplacement of the material had a probable gun, but the amount of material was long done by the men. The temporary loophole of timber also caused trouble as a labour shortage of loading. Here is a forward loophole to meet immediate need. The strength pattern was not sufficient to cope with all the work in hand, without having a reserve. Upon the men had to be commenced on the men and infantry assistance was not available. There a new dug out had to be commenced near the flame, and a considerable shift of men required, and no men came up. The expansion of improvement schemes during this time was the gradual production of cartridge supplies to hold bombs ready for all to protect the gun further.

Marked progress was made in protection against enemy's attack for bombing parties answering this day being fitted out as Jeoffroi. Rifle having steel spring thermals. The equipment of the whole unit with the new iron roller equipment sheets was also effected, and the use of this being explained to the detachment who were also practised for the subject from time to time (date too late) secured and assigned to all the positions in the line (and various men to know ready and forward).

Army Form C. 2118.

WAR DIARY
or
INTELLIGENCE SUMMARY.
(Erase heading not required.)

Instructions regarding War Diaries and Intelligence Summaries are contained in F. S. Regs., Part II. and the Staff Manual respectively. Title pages will be prepared in manuscript.

Place	Date	Hour	Summary of Events and Information	Remarks and references to Appendices
MESNIL			During the second week of the month, it was still necessary to expend ammunition with care, and apart from any targets engaged at the request of the Infantry or by orders from Artillery groups, only short unobtrusive shoots were carried out to keep the enemy T.M. with destructive intent. On the 9th, various shoots (23) were fired for registration of S.O.S lines and for retaliation upon a hostile M.T.M. east of	
	9.7.18	3.15–3.30		
		9.30 a.m		
	10.7.18	3 p.m–4.30 p.m	Monday a destructive shoot was undertaken by enemy batteries. Directed on release against a small group of enemy mortars, co/25 TMB bombarded the enemy group with D.25 Lbs LbS with	See S.I.D. N.Z.
		6.45 p.m	any of 36 the nest m 2.35d two rounds TM was all 58 rounds, and immediately following, ceasing, the retaliatory following sheetan amount of enemy's a rail sweeping fire was directed by us upon 2.35d in suff of a mail by a T.M.B. on the 11th July. On the 12th nothing	
	11.7.18			
	12.7.18		Thursday only a small shoot was executed. No group's return	
	13.7.18		hostile O.M's x 2.35 a t.b but this was unmolesting in day's new position. Our was neared on the mortar group, another after unsuccessful attempts with K.I.C.M. to with a sheelle and lost, but loss the place of the mortar until to employed. The target engaged necessitated a maximum angle of 15° and the use of the S.A. charge, and the new position gives access the stone wall.	

WAR DIARY or INTELLIGENCE SUMMARY

Army Form C. 2118.

Place	Date	Hour	Summary of Events and Information	Remarks and references to Appendices
MESNIL			There were at this time many indications that an enemy attack might at any time be launched against this or a neighbouring front, and so the Defence of the area must prove very difficult to resist hostility. The greatest efforts must now be made for trench works, and the overall defence scheme endeavoured. Orders of the Corps and Divisional Artillery Commanders, a regulation from Mont Fautin was set on foot. The greatest possible demand for the armament of mortars in the journal and should be reduced, and that a series of guns should be equipped with this scheme of armament. The mass line of defence. The huts should be put into a group of COURT line was carried out, and rest ridden for a group of war-emplacements for each battery according which sent out of the line on the 10th July were employed for two days upon the digging of these emplacements, and had two days rest before moving into the hold into their positions, from where downwards the enemy gun rifle ground. The valley in front of the Huple line could be swept by with a view to the strongest defence of that line on or in front of which the Corps Commander had resolved to hold out the fall. In conjunction with this great disposition of mortars every precaution was taken on the already moving implements to ensure the rapid and effective manning of the guns should an attack develop. Entries were distributed, including preparation for instant action was maintained.	

Army Form C. 2118.

WAR DIARY
or
INTELLIGENCE SUMMARY.
(Erase heading not required.)

Instructions regarding War Diaries and Intelligence Summaries are contained in F. S. Regs., Part II. and the Staff Manual respectively. Title pages will be prepared in manuscript.

Place	Date	Hour	Summary of Events and Information	Remarks and references to Appendices
MENIN	14.7.16		off the same time so far as was possible improvements were effected on the existing emplacements, and the road leading to Zero and approaches was continued. Our second line positions without Menin as reserve were renamed "Intermediate" and those under Consumeter to the rear received their former name of "Reserve". Preparations was made in Zone to attack Zoo-trophy farms, including Foret W.11. Munro-Stuart for the sudden, was told yet available. Bombardment, also, was short, and guns and men had to be employed in some instances to save the casualties you occurred. The enemy attack, expected to materialise at some time in the following week, failed to do so, and the whole situation remained unchanged. On the 14th, a further hostile artillery ... referred to above was carried out. 3 rounds were fired from a hostile howitzer P.M.s in ~235 H.e., this being apparently a calibre of 8.2" — those of high charge I also found that he that (or the howitzer which were ambushed for keeps or not at any) (If the troops advanced, but that the next shoes might be of (sent a firing however, but that was made of high tempered steel, advantage of the shell was made of high tempered steel. Mt Gray 15 rounds were fired upon Ozone Line to cogs and exploded Recheli window every shoot modelled tamely.	
15.7.16				

Army Form C. 2118.

WAR DIARY
or
INTELLIGENCE SUMMARY.
(Erase heading not required.)

Instructions regarding War Diaries and Intelligence Summaries are contained in F. S. Regs., Part II. and the Staff Manual respectively. Title pages will be prepared in manuscript.

Place	Date	Hour	Summary of Events and Information	Remarks and references to Appendices
MESNIL	15.7.18	5-6.30pm	and took were specially hit, and after wards worked sthg & our trenches which carried out after our mortars and filled to the extent of 30 rounds in all. Enemy retaliated as usual until the time, not comparably later, amounting only to 30 rounds 77mm shell.	
	16.7.18 to 6.45pm	The enemy replied to a shoot of 20 rounds carried out by No 1 L/T mi of his mortars with four rounds of 77mm shell first ranging 50 in front of the mortar position. Hostile mortars were again engaged on the 19th and on the 20th in each case as a retaliatory reply provided.	
	17.7.18/7.30pm to 8pm		
	16.7.18 3pm	During these days progress was made in the new positions held by battalions in the line. Lashings "tote" was obtained, and the greater part of our trenches were provided with ample dermate triple protective curtain to the end of the week. Progress was made with the new reserve emplacements on the Rifle System. This was affected on...	

Now 21.7.18 affording completion of support the revetment, and the gradual improvement of support these revetments, and the further use of equipment and occupied areas.

WAR DIARY

Army Form C. 2118.

Place: MESNIL

Date	Hour	Summary of Events and Information	Remarks and references to Appendices
23.7.16 28.7.16		Should be noted that on the 18th the approximate strength of holding the line was increased by Coys. of the Infantry on the centre Division, who had orders to be used tactically, and the hill + right divisions who ordered to be used, if any of the Bn's. was depleted to fill the gap. Our left Sector (at 35 & 37) was and under gas tactical control of 87 T.M.O. B.T.M.B. Gas and our right Sector under that of 97 & 70 17 Div. Ammunition and communication supply, carriers concerned in this was of 97 T.M.O. 35 Div.	
		The situation remained very quiet during the last month of the month. The left and right batteries were still under the control of the 63rd Div. and 17 Div. T.M.O.'s respectively, who served as regards ammunition gun expenditure + ammunition, and don't find dumps, relief of personnel etc.	
24.7.16 5pm		The usual run of fire. On the 26 or onwards relieving he was carried out by 97.35 upon 50 area from which heavy T.M. fire was away on the left and dense of trench T.M.'s afterwards of TM refuses. He was very of this occasion. to further thought then attempted of the new "Gun" position so to longer in the line was the completion of the new "Gun" position south the time was the sap of 97.38 T.M.B. There were several shown as far and this was especially near of 97.38 T.M.B.	
25.7.16		And retaliated in every way as heavily as possible, and on the left	

Army Form C. 2118.

WAR DIARY
or
INTELLIGENCE SUMMARY.
(Erase heading not required.)

Instructions regarding War Diaries and Intelligence Summaries are contained in F. S. Regs., Part II. and the Staff Manual respectively. Title pages will be prepared in manuscript.

Place	Date	Hour	Summary of Events and Information	Remarks and references to Appendices
MESNIL	26.7.18		A mittorlos Pskm active in O/Khour. A letter to my supervised the ENGLEBEIMER to reconnoitre the detachment of a reconnaissance district. On the 30th of July an amount was again made to move up preparation for an attack which was today. The guns were established at a forward point of 3/35 from the date at G/38 1a to surprise and local advance arrived arranged.	
	30.7.18		On this date the batteries fired under the orders of either one of the 2 O.3 in conjunction with 5 heavy trenches. A total of 330 rounds from 2/35 T.M.B.) and 1/4 (Mortar of Heavy shells from 2/23 to 4 rounds (1/35 T.M.B.) In the afternoon on the comp of the enemy (2/35 T.M.B.) In the afternoon on the comp of our battery, and Battery were relieved by 63 & D.N.Low TMB and marched to H.Q.N of VARENNES the following day and commenced re-organisation & refitting prior to a period of intensive training.	
VARENNES HERISSART	31.7.18			

O J Fowler
Lt. R.F.A.
2/7/90 35th Bde

31.7.18

Army Form C. 2118.

WAR DIARY
or
INTELLIGENCE SUMMARY.
(Erase heading not required.)

Instructions regarding War Diaries and Intelligence Summaries are contained in F. S. Regs., Part II. and the Staff Manual respectively. Title pages will be prepared in manuscript.

Place	Date	Hour	Summary of Events and Information	Remarks and references to Appendices
			Casualties	
	6-7-18		1 O.R. Killed in action	
	12-7-18		Lt P.W Taub's RFA to Hosp. Hun. Sac. 12.7.18	
	8-7-18 to 25-7-18		Capt F.P Stevenson RFA granted leave to U.K	
	22-7-18		2/Lieut Smith RFA attached to Fourth Army M. School	
	19-7-18		2/Lt Little RFA seconded to Second Army M. School	

Army Form C. 2118.

WAR DIARY
or
INTELLIGENCE SUMMARY.
(Erase heading not required.)

WAR DIARY – AUGUST 1918.

38th Divisional Trench Mortar Batteries

WAR DIARY
or
INTELLIGENCE SUMMARY.

Army Form C. 2118.

(Erase heading not required.)

Instructions regarding War Diaries and Intelligence Summaries are contained in F. S. Regs., Part II. and the Staff Manual respectively. Title pages will be prepared in manuscript.

Place	Date	Hour	Summary of Events and Information	Remarks and references to Appendices
SENLIS MARTINSART BOUZINCOURT MESNIL	9/3/18	Sheet 57D	Location Martinsart. Three officers and 881 other ranks as shown. Affiliated. The three sub sections at present in SENLIS where an officer supervised the H.Q. detachments at BOUZINCOURT & MARTINSART. I learnt officer explored from MESNIL MOUND the two detachments at MESNIL. Equipment was maintained, explosives repaired and communication checked and kept engaged the course of instruction by his section till the middle of the month.	Appendix I
	14.6.18			
	19.8.18		By this date the enemy was already showing his retirement on our front and reconnaissance was made for offensive positions as those hitherto need had not now sufficient range to deal with the enemy. Next day this latter were followed to Henenpul its defences furnished and collect all intact. This gathered at at central point for unkeping use. The activities of the tapperies can again be noted	
	20.8.18		heights from this front	

WAR DIARY
or
INTELLIGENCE SUMMARY.
(Erase heading not required.)

Army Form C. 2118.

Place	Date	Hour	Summary of Events and Information	Remarks and references to Appendices
HERLOCOURT	1.1.18		Sheet 57d.	
	2.8.18		[illegible handwritten entries]	
VARENNES 66.18				
HEDAUVILLE 7.8.18				

Z 3 8 T M B/5

Vol 1

apr '16
may '16

WAR DIARY
or
INTELLIGENCE SUMMARY.

Army Form C. 2118.

(Erase heading not required.)

Instructions regarding War Diaries and Intelligence Summaries are contained in F. S. Regs., Part II. and the Staff Manual respectively. Title pages will be prepared in manuscript.

Place	Date	Hour	Summary of Events and Information	Remarks and references to Appendices
MESSINES			Sheet 57B S.E.	
	5/6/15	12/35 TM/15	The Battery commenced at MESSINES was ordered out early this morning to take the f... on B.23 T.7.13. on arrival at billets the remainder of Battery following today. All of the Battery having been placed in action at M.29.d.21.d.32. Under the action of M.29.d.31.d.32. Tigers, near gun at one gun... Officer... Battery commenced action, and firing was commenced & the rate of the normal firing shortly but ceased target at L.23.d.1. Normal unless the enemy are... this time maintaining strong fire... ... commenced fire at enemy trenches which ... ... his trenches are to the former position at the front...	
	7/6/15		The PURPLE SYSTEM from M.13.b. that of Battery 29.k B... ... B 26 a 3.3 ... ... the action of one Officer per section	
	10/6/15			
	12/6/15			
		A.F.A.	By this date the enemy was already commencing his retirement, and had withdrawn to the Huber Tusch. The officer of C/35 therefore recognized for ... positions at L 29.a.3.,5. ... nd of 21 New Jerky, kept it ... to found impracticable to maintain guns in action there.	

WAR DIARY or INTELLIGENCE SUMMARY

Army Form C. 2118.

Place	Date	Hour	Summary of Events and Information	Remarks and references to Appendices
	28/5/18		Sheet 57.D. S.E. The narratives regarding the two battles seem again to be completed from this front. The enemy's retirement being in progress French Motors became available, and the greater part of the unit was turned to this purpose.	
	29/5/18		Even on the 22nd a party of 1 Officer and 30 O.R's reported to 8.F.C. for work to the M.R.F. Oct. 1 S.A. 9.E., and on the 24th 12 gunners reported to 162.222 Bde to replace casualties. In the same date Lewis gunners were distributed by the unit to the Brigades and Div. Inf. Headquarters. 16 party and 4 Offrs were employed upon an aeroplane another 16 party and 4 Offrs (four Officers) was made to fly mgts of the Div. etc. (four Officers) On the 26th the Headquarters of the Unit had been moved to Sulys. On the 28th they went again advanced to Bois Kelly, W24, and on the 29th to the edge of Marcy Wood. (Sheet 57(C). On the 31st a party of one Officer and 5 O.R returned to the areas from which M had advanced, and collected at MACENNES the guns and stores which these had then neither the time nor the necessary transport to remove. It seems with a mobile mortar Bgy still in action when the month closed but this unit	
	30/5/18			
	31/5/18		dry/ished. Up to whatever is, which it was subjected to, its embargo employment, one described in appendix	

WAR DIARY
INTELLIGENCE SUMMARY
(Erase heading not required.)

Army Form C. 2118.

Place	Date	Hour	Summary of Events and Information	Remarks and references to Appendices
Reference Map Sheet France 57 D S.E.			Location Post: Y/38/T.M.B.	Appendix I.
Location Bat: X/38/T.M.B.			H.Q. V 3 D 68	
H.Q. Q 28 a 95.65			Sectn H.2 V 10 D 95 20	
Emplacements			Q 28 D 20 10	
Q 22 D 28 15 ⎫			Emplacements — Mag Bearings — S.O.S Targets	
Q 22 D 28 20 ⎬ Offensive			W 13 a 60 15 ⎫ BOUZINCOURT 148° — W 20 a 55 15	
Q 22 D 20 02 ⎬			W 13 a 3 6 ⎭ 133° — W 14 c 65 20	
Q 22 D 20 05 ⎭			W 3 c 15 50 ⎫ MARTINSART 143° — W 10 c 00 95	
Q 27 a 06 86 ⎫			W 3 c 15 75 ⎭ 104° — W 14 c 50 35	
Q 21 a 37 10 ⎬ Defensive			W 34 b 21 80 ⎫ MESNIL 93° — Q 35 d 45 90	
Q 21 a 37 20 ⎭			W 34 b 46 38 ⎭ 121° — Q 35 d 40 90	
Q 22 D 20 85 New Offensive position				

WAR DIARY or INTELLIGENCE SUMMARY

Army Form C. 2118.

Place	Date	Hour	Summary of Events and Information	Remarks and references to Appendices
457C			Mobile Trench Mortars (6" Newton)	
	23/8/16		On Aug. 23, in the open country between VARENNES & HEDAUVILLE trial was made of a device intended to aid our carriers landing into fascine and uneven ground, especially in offensive warfare, to the 6" NEWTON (stationary) L.S. fed umrotation, and provided with pads & the under-side. For this a low trolley was supplied, with strong iron frame to support the bed. The trolley looks on behind set ordinary to trailer, in which ammunition can be carried, the mortar can be mounted on the bed (time compiled) to the day of trial, the bed worked quite well, although connected filled to one side, and actual firing was carried out. The possibility of the use of such mortars being indicated than for a party of Officers 1 Sgt. 3 GMS. + 10 Gunners moved off a 25/1/5 pm. SENLIS for the line, the arm being to keep in touch with and assist the advancing Infantry. Two 6" trailers with mortars attached were taken, and 2 ISHrs with ammunition. The first move was to place lorry in BSHEFONS well e/ammunition. On the night of the 26th/27th the party advanced to CONTALMAISON LONGUEVAL ROAD, and in the course of the 27th adjourned on CONTALMAISON VILLA, and on the 27th into position to belly overing to a temporary check but could not come into belly, owing to a temporary check sustained by the Infantry, we returned to CONTALMAISON VILLA.	
	26/27	8.15		

Army Form C. 2118.

WAR DIARY
or
INTELLIGENCE SUMMARY.
(Erase heading not required.)

Instructions regarding War Diaries and Intelligence Summaries are contained in F. S. Regs., Part II. and the Staff Manual respectively. Title pages will be prepared in manuscript.

Place	Date	Hour	Summary of Events and Information	Remarks and references to Appendices
Sheet 5	21/8/16 29/8/16		Appendix 11 See 9th	
	31/8/16		Next day the party returned to LONGUEVAL and in the early morning of the 29th fired on DELVILLE WOOD in the y'ground which was LONGUEVAL. He was informed to, and GINCHY. Forty rounds were fired. The SSteel of me mortar that that being during use. Unfortunately first were employed the 113 R.J. Bde was then relieved, to which the party had been attached and quarters a short distance in rear of Longueval were occupied. Orders for further arrangements to take on MORVAL. Guns ammunition was taken forward, but the shoot was cancelled at the last moment.	

O C Trench
Bght. R.F.A.
A.J.M.O.
38th (WELSH) DIV.

Army Form C. 2118.

WAR DIARY
or
INTELLIGENCE SUMMARY.
(Erase heading not required.)

Instructions regarding War Diaries and Intelligence Summaries are contained in F. S. Regs., Part II. and the Staff Manual respectively. Title pages will be prepared in manuscript.

Place	Date	Hour	Summary of Events and Information	Remarks and references to Appendices
			Casualties:	
	1/8/18		2 ORs from Hospital	
	4/8/18		1 OR. to hospital sick	
			1 OR. to hospital accidentally injured	
	6/8/18		1 OR to hospital accidentally injured	
			1 OR to hospital sick	
	8/8/18		1 OR from hospital	
	12/8/18		1 OR from hospital	
	13/8/18		1 OR to hospital sick	
	14/8/18		1 OR to hospital sick	
	19/8/18		1 OR from hospital	
	21/8/18		22 J.F. Little to hospital sick & evacuated to England	
	22/8/18		1 OR to hospital sick	
	24/8/18		1 OR from hospital	

Army Form C. 2118.

WAR DIARY
or
INTELLIGENCE SUMMARY.
(Erase heading not required.)

WAR DIARY - SEPTEMBER 1918

38TH DIVISIONAL TRENCH MORTAR BATTERIES.

WAR DIARY
or
INTELLIGENCE SUMMARY.

(Erase heading not required.)

Army Form C. 2118.

Place	Date	Hour	Summary of Events and Information	Remarks and references to Appendices
MAMETZ	1.9.16		Sheet 57C	
	2.9.16		On Sept 1. 97MO's HQRS were moved Mametz Wood, and the Section with Mobile Workshops moved to GINCHY. This Section remained at Ginchy. The following day, and HQRS were moved to LONGUEVAL. On the 3rd the Mobile Sections moved to MORVAL. T11 d 30.10. etc orders were received	Casualties Appendix I.
LONGUEVAL MORVAL NURLU COURT	3.9.16		attaching it to the forward Brigade. it now moved to MANANCOURT	
			U10 d, 9, 7. No targets were assigned in those days	
	5.9.16		On this date orders were received transferring the division to the command of C.R.A. 17"Div. The Mobile Section Bus Trenches Detachment	
			to LONGUEVAL, and personnel of 3S "TM B's still remaining (and not otherwise employed within the Div Hdqrs) joined the 6th Div	
	6.9.16		On the 7th the unit marched to LE SARS (M19 c) and the two	
LE SARS	7.9.16		following days were also passed there. On the 10th the unit marched to ROCQUIGNY and camped by the Light Railway Station. On the 11th a move was made to a Shelter camp at BUS. On this date	
ROCQUIGNY	10.9.16			
BUS	11.9.16		the Mobile Section of the unit was placed under the orders of 115 SY Bde. and marched to P 35 d 5, 2. to reconnoitre actions in the time with the Div Infantry. The 97MO reported at B.A. on same date to do temporary duty as Staff Captain, but next day received orders to reassemble	
	12.9.16		the entire unit in readiness for action. Orders were issued and preparations made to this end.	

WAR DIARY or INTELLIGENCE SUMMARY

Army Form C. 2118.

Place	Date	Hour	Summary of Events and Information	Remarks and references to Appendices
EQUANCOURT	13.9.18		Lieut 37 C.	
			On the 13th Minfor, Officers and OR's who had been sent to Brigade HQrs, Batteries and DHQ assembled at EQUANCOURT to which TMB HQrs moved from BUS on this date. (V.10.B.1.5.) The TMO reported the same morning. TMB reported there for duties, as did one officer + 5 OR's from the Heavy Heavy T.M.B., who were to man German LEICHTE MINENWERFER also under TMO. 38 his LEICHTE M.W. was told the evening and details of plans worked out. That day OMO's HQRS was moved forward to P.35.c.5.2. and reconnaissance was made by officers of the line, and gun positions, ammunition dumps, Battery HQ and rendezvous for carrying parties selected. Targets were allocated for the impending attack, under cover of which the Division was to get the night guns and ammunition were got to the forward area as under:-	Further details regarding the Battery are shown in
	14.9.18			Appendix II a) Location b) Spare Battery
			c/32 TMB 3 guns complete 300 rds T.M.E. 7/35 " 6 " 340 " " 7/17 " 3 " 100 " " 4 MINENWERFER 300 " M.W. ammunition. 6" NEWTON MORTARS on the line, 8 MINENWERFER Section from 7/17	c) Transport Table
			Preparations aimed at having 18 6" NEWTON MORTARS in the line, 8 MINENWERFER plus 1000 rds Minenwerfer ammunition, the	

Army Form C. 2118.

WAR DIARY
or
INTELLIGENCE SUMMARY.
(Erase heading not required.)

Instructions regarding War Diaries and Intelligence Summaries are contained in F. S. Regs., Part II. and the Staff Manual respectively. Title pages will be prepared in manuscript.

Place	Date	Hour	Summary of Events and Information	Remarks and references to Appendices
EQUANCOURT	14.9.18		Sheet 57c. ammunition to be expended on a bombardment of 1 hrs duration. The main targets were ZOWLAND HEATHER & AFRICAN TRENCHES and those immediately defending GOUZEAU COURT. Next day a modification of the Div. front line was necessitating a modification of the scheme for mortars. 17th Div. took over the left sector of 38 Div. front on the SOUTH, and 38 Div. extended its frontage NORTHWARDS for a short distance. To avoid unnecessary work & shemie on the part of defending Batteries 3/1/17 TMB did not for the morning move onto the front of its own Div. but dealt under ATMO 38 Div. & 2/35 TMB whilst already had guns in the area now held by 17 Div. worked under DTMB 17 Div. On Mistake Guns were taken forward as	appendix II
"	15.9.18		under 3/1/17 6 6" NEWTONS Section 2/1/5 4 additional MINENWERFER 2/35 3 6" NEWTONS The locations of guns are set out in appendix II a) It proved that two days remained for preparation. These were occupied in getting mortars and ammunition into position. Working parties of Infantry were used during this period, as the necessary concentration could not	1) Working Party Tables. 4)
"	16.9.18			

Army Form C. 2118.

WAR DIARY
or
INTELLIGENCE SUMMARY.
(Erase heading not required.)

Place	Date	Hour	Summary of Events and Information	Remarks and references to Appendices
EQUANCOURT	17.9.18		Sheet 57.C.	
			On this date the GHQMB moved forward to Bn HQRS at 74A 1.5 in order to be made advanced Q.H. and in a position to control the T.M. Batteries. Early next day a further move to Q34 a 1.3 was made, the latter location having proved more convenient. A fresh distribution of targets has been made, these being divided between Y35 ~~to take the two largest positions~~ Y/17 & Y/35 T.M.B. While the fire of the Section employing MINENWERFER was by the Sturmpionier on many of the objectives. The targets were sunken roads & trenches immediately	Appendix II (5)
GOUZEAUCOURT SECTOR	18.9.15		in front of GOUZEAUCOURT.	
		5.20 A.M.	ZERO hour was 5.20 A.M. The T.M Batteries took part in the bombardment each target receiving attention for a specified time. 501 rounds T.M.B were expended, and about 300 MINEN. The effectiveness of the latter was impaired by heavy rain, which had affected much ⊥, and rendered undiscoverable. The remainder of the M.M. ammunition available. Enemy counter fire was weak, and resulted in casualties shown in Appendix I. A further supply of 6" NEWTON ammunition was taken forward at night 19/35 and 9/17 T.M.Bs exchanged positions similar to in the course of the day.	Appendix I

WAR DIARY or INTELLIGENCE SUMMARY

Army Form C. 2118.

Place	Date	Hour	Summary of Events and Information	Remarks and references to Appendices
ROCQUIGNY (H.Q. for GUZEAUCOURT SECTOR)	24/9/18		The batteries were put at the disposal of 97TMO 17 Div. for approaching operations. Orders were received regarding fire situations. Our mortars were to be placed in positions as shown in Appendix III	Further details of these operations are shown in Appendix III
	25/9/18		SUPPORT and 2 mobile mortars were also to be employed. On this date, Menfort, 3 guns complete of 97F & 96F TMB were carried forward, together with 50 rds ammunition. Preliminary situation was ordered for the early morning of the 27.9.18, to be the zero hour from Q.35.a central to Q.29.e.90.50. Our mortars were ordered before a zero hour	
	26/9/18		a) Q.35.a and Q.29.d. b) are complete & put battery were later formed, and B40 rds ammunition. Infantry parties moved for each battery all morning and from 5pm & 9pm also (1st, 2nd & 3rd) Working party Inf 1st div. 7/35 respectively	a) Reinforced b) Transport details
	27/9/18		Zero hour was 9.52 a.m. The two mobile mortars forced in the first line of the enemy in Q.35.a. & Q.29.c. The remaining guns engaged for a like purpose - No Z.28.b.20, strategic points Q.35.a.26. Q.29.a.26. Q.29.d. Q.30.c. In sunken road a Q.35.a.26.	
EQUANCOURT	28/9/18		97TMO's HQRS moved from Q.29 d.2.2 to Y.17 b.	
	29/9/18		Batteries moved from the line to the above HQRS guns, lewis & platforms being taken by motor lorries to H.23.d, angle between Railway & Road.	
	30/9/18		Unit by rail at Y.17.b.	*

O. J. Simmons
Capt. R.F.A.
97TMO. 35 Div.

WAR DIARY
or
INTELLIGENCE SUMMARY.

Army Form C. 2118.

Place	Date	Hour	Summary of Events and Information	Remarks and references to Appendices
GOUZEAU-COURT SECTOR	18/9/18		Sheet 57 C. During the fluctuations of the battle the following bombardments were also carried out. 2/17 TMB & the detachment with Minenwerfers fired on Q.35.a.50.50 and AFRICAN TRENCH.	
"	"	2.5pm	2/17 engaged Q.35.a 60.50.	
"	19/9/18		Coy 35 TMB fired upon AFRICAN TRENCH from Q.35.a.70 to Q.29.c.95.50. This was laid out on Q.29.c.85.00 and Q.29.d.76.42.	
"	20/9/18		On the morning of this date reconnaissance was carried out in order to select more advanced emplacements from which to engage the enemy line at Q.35.a.34.45 the sector from Q.35.a. 50 75 to Q.29.d.00.45. The same night 2/35 covered 113 Bde. which had relieved 113 Bde in left sector, and 2/35 covered 50 Bde. which had relieved 114 Bde in right sector. 2/35 TMB withdrew to billets at EQUANCOURT on this date.	
	21.9.18		17 TMB moved to headquarters hut to EQUANCOURT. During the night 2/35 TMB was also withdrawn relieved by 17 TMB & withdrew to EQUANCOURT.	
Rocquigny	22.9.18		The whole unit marched to near ROCQUIGNY O.29.d.2.2.	
	23.9.18		was spent at ROCQUIGNY.	

Appendix I CASUALTIES.

Sheet 57c.

X/38 TM BATTERY

date	name No.		nature of casualty
18/9/18	2/Lt	W.J. Todd RFA	Wounded in action
19/9/18		-do-	died of Wounds
17/9/18	253753	Gr. McCartney RFA	Wounded in action
18/9/18	74092	A/Corpl Burrel S. RFA	killed in action
"	5530	" Burrell G.H. RFA	Wounded in action
"	5330	Gr. Salter H	"
"	201385	" Sampson E	"
9/9/18	83785	" Tinworth J	"
19/9/18	63695	" Rice BJ	"
18/9/18	283	B! Povrnham	"

Y/38 TM BATTERY.

date	name No.		nature of casualty
15/9/18	1395	Gp. F Road RFA	Wounded in action

Appendix II (a)

LOCATION LIST

D.T.M.Os. H.Q. P35 d 5.2 — Advance H.Q. W 4 a 15.

WAGON LINE — V 10 B 13

Sheet 57c.

BATTERY	H.Q.	EMPLACEMENTS	DUMP	RENDEZVOUS FOR WORKING PARTIES
X/38 T.M. BATTERY	W 10 B 60.65	W 4 D 17.00 (1) W 5 C 00.90 (2) W 10 B 60.65 (3)	W 10 B 60.65	W 10 B 60.65 (where roadway crosses sunken road)
Y/38 T.M. Battery	W 3 A 30.15	W 4 B 15.75 W 4 B 20.75 W 4 B 15.70 W 4 B 25.70 W 4 B 30.70 W 4 B 80.70	W 3 B 55.95	W 3 a 50.25
Y/17 T.M. Battery	Q 34 c 60.30	Q 34 D 38.38 Q 34 D 40.40 Q 34 A 45.45 Q 34 A 45.50 Q 34 A 48.58 Q 34 B 55.55	Q 34 D 40 35 9 W 4 B 00 70	W 4 a 10 50 (Bn/n H.Q.)
M.W. Detachment V/N T.M. Battery	Q 34 D 50.60	Q 34 D 70.10 (4) Q 34 D 70 70 (4)	Q 34 D 50 60	Q 34 D 50 60.

Appendix II (6)
Sheet 57c.
SECRET

38th DIVISIONAL T.M. BATTERIES.
ORDER No 1.

1. X/38 T.M.B., Y/38 T.M.B., Y/17 T.M.B. and Minenwerfer Section of V/V TMB. will be concentrated at EQUANCOURT V 10 c 18. on 13th and 14th September and will go into action on the front of 38th Division on nights 14th/15th and 15th/16th. Three mortars per 6" T.M Battery and first group of 4 light minenwerfer must be in action with 100 rounds per gun at emplacement by 4.0 A.M. 16th September and all mortars must be in action with 100 rounds per gun by 4.0 A.M. 17th September.

2. Targets are allotted as follows:-
   X/38 T.M.B. - LOWLAND and HEATHER TRENCHES in W 11 c and W 5 D.
   Y/38 T.M.B. - HEATHER and AFRICAN TRENCHES in W 5 B. and Q 35 C. and TRENCH in W 6 A. and Q 36 C.
   Y/17 T.M.B. - AFRICAN TRENCH in Q 35 and the GOUZEAUCOURT DEFENCES in Q 35 and Q 36.

   MW detachment V/V TMB: - 1st Group of 4 guns to fire on GOUZEAUCOURT DEFENCES in Q 35 D and Q 36.
   " - 2nd Group of 4 guns to fire on HEATHER and LOWLAND TRENCHES in W 5 and W 11 B.

   Enfilade fire will be arranged for as follows:-
   X/38 T.M.B. - 2 guns to engage HEATHER TRENCH W 5 D 15.18 and W 5 D 00.50
   Y/17 T.M.B. - 2 guns to engage AFRICAN TRENCH 2 35 a. 60.60. to 2 35 a. 55.30.

3. Reconnaissances will be carried out by Battery Commanders on the 14th September for the following:-
   1. Positions for guns.
   2. Battery ammunition dumps. (These must be kept distinct and should be on the FINS - GOUZEAUCOURT ROAD)
   3. Battery Rendesvous for ammunition carrying parties.
   4. Route for carrying parties from Battery Dumps to emplacements.
   5. Accommodation for Battery H.Qs. detachments.
   6. Telephone communication between Battery H.Qs. and Battalion H.Qs. at W 4 a 1.4 or W 33 central.

   Reports on Reconnaissances must be forwarded to D.T.M.O. by 3.30 P.M.

Appendix II G
Sheet 57c

4. **Ammunition Supply.** A Dump for T.M. ammunition is being formed at V6B.9.7. Ammunition will be brought here by lorry and taken forward by G.S. wagons.
Battery Commanders must arrange to supply the following nightly:—
1. Guides for transport from V6B. to Battery Dump.
2. Unloading party at Battery Dump.
3. Officer to meet infantry carrying party and to lead them to emplacements.
Detail will be issued daily from D.T.M.O's office.

5. **Ration and Water supply.** This will be carried out through Q.M.S. 38th Div. T.M. Batteries.
Battery Commanders will report to him by 6 p.m. daily
1. Ration strength of detachments in the line
2. Ration strength of Battery exclusive of above.
Rations and water will be sent up on ammunition wagons.

6. 38th D.T.M.O's H.Q. will move to P35 D 5.2 at 10 A.M. on 14th September.

Issued at 7 A.M.
14-9-18.

J Stewart
Capt R.F.A.
D.T.M.O. 38th Division.

Copies to:
X/38 T.M.B.
Y/38 T.M.B.
Y/17 T.M.B.
M.W. Detachment
V/V T.M.B.
38th D.A.
T.M. Officer Vth Corps R.A.
File.

2.

Appendix II c.
Sheet 57c

38" Divisional Trench Mortar Batteries

DETAIL OF TRANSPORT for night 14th/15th Sept.

BATTERY	NO. OF WAGONS	UNIT SUPPLYING TRANSPORT	RENDEZVOUS	TIME	NATURE OF WORK	REMARKS
MW Detachment V T.M. Battery	2	38th Div. T.M. Battery	V10 B 1.5.	6.30 p.m.	Transport of guns from EQUANCOURT & ammunition from V6 B 97 to Battery Dump - 2 journeys.	Loading and unloading parties must be supplied by Batteries & carrying parties are required to arrive at Battery Dumps by that time.
X38 T.M. Battery	2	38th D.A.C.	V 6 B 97	6.30 p.m.	Transport of Ammunition to Battery Dump - 2 journeys.	
	2	38th D.A.C.	V 10 B 1.8	6.30 p.m.	Transport of guns to Battery Dump 1 journey.	
Y38 T.M. Battery	ao for X/38		T.M. Battery			
Y17 T.M. Battery	ao for X/38		T.M. Battery			

Note:- Battery Commanders will arrange for Rations and Water for detachments in the line to be sent up on above wagons.

Sheet 57c

38TH DIVISIONAL T.M. BATTERIES   Appendix II 6

Operation Order No 3

Reference enclosed R.A.G.S. 251/19 dated 17-9-18

1. Y/38 T.M. Battery will engage targets 1-6 Y/17 targets 7-12 and V/V TM Battery targets 2-4-5-6-7-9-10-11.

2. Synchronisation of watches will take place at 9.0 pm at Q 34 d 40 60.

3. At conclusion of shooting Batteries will remain in action in readiness for counter-attack; one officer and two detachments of each Battery will be kept ready to move forward in order to bring captured Mortars into action

4. D.T.M.O. will establish his H.Q. at W 4 a 15 at 6.0 pm.

(Sd) O.J. Jones.

Capt. RFA.
D.T.M.O 38TH DIV.

Issued at 3.0 pm.
17-9-18.

Sheet 57/c   Appendix II L
                                              SECRET.

38th Divl T.M. Batteries

ORDER No 2.

1. Owing to rearrangement of Divisional Boundaries, X/38 T.M.B. will come under orders of D.T.M.O. 17th Div. with effect from 15th Sept.

2. Targets on new front of 38th Division are now allotted as follows:-

   Y/38 T.M.B. — Trenches and sunken roads in the area — W5 b 70 55 - W6 a 70 90 - Q 36 c 35 95 - Q 35 b 55 00.

   Y/17 T.M.B. — Trenches and sunken roads in the area — Q 35 b 55 00 - Q 36 c 35 95 - Q 30 c 15 25 - Q 29 d 60 50.

   Minenwerfer Section of V/V T.M.B. will bring 4 guns to bear on each of the above areas.

3. X/38 T.M.B. will exchange three mortars with Y/17 T.M.B.

4. <u>Ammunition</u> allotment is reduced to 50 rounds per 6" T.M.

                                        O J Jones
                                        Capt R.F.A.
15. 9. 18   D.T.M.O. 38th Div.
Issued at 7.0 pm.

Copies to:-
  X/38 T.M.B.   V/V T.M.B.
  Y/38 T.M.B.   38th Div. Arty.
  Y/17 T.M.B.   T.M. Officer Vth Corps R.A.

Army Form C. 2118.

WAR DIARY
or
INTELLIGENCE SUMMARY.
(Erase heading not required.)

Sheet 57c. Appendix II c.

TRANSPORT TABLES. 15-9-18.

BATTERY	No. OF WAGONS	UNIT SUPPLYING	RENDEZVOUS	TIME	NATURE OF WORK.
V/5	2	38 bw T M Bs	V.10.b.1.8	6 pm	Carrying MWs from V.10.b.1.8 & V.6.c.9.7 & ammunition to positions 2 journeys
Y.17	2	38 DAC.	38 bw ARP.	6.30 pm	Carrying 6" TMs from ARP. & TM DUMP to positions

Appendix II d
Sheet 57c

38TH DIVISION TRENCH MORTAR BATTERIES.
WORKING PARTY TABLE. 14/15-9-18

Serial No.	Strength of Party	Supplied by	Rendezvous	Time	To be met by	Nature of work	Remarks
A	1 Officer 20 men	14 RWF	V.3.a.50.25	8-30 PM 14-9-18	Officer & X/38 T.M.B.	Carrying Ammn 3 journeys	As these 3 parties report together Battery representatives will meet them together and arrange distribution amongst themselves
B	1 Officer 20 men	"	"	"	Officer & Y/38 T.M.B.	"	
C	1 Officer 20 men	"	"	"	Officer & Y/14 T.M.B.	"	
D	1 NCO 9 men	"	"	8-0 AM 15-9-18	Officer & X/38 T.M.B.	ditto 5 journeys	
E	1 NCO 9 men	"	"	"	Officer & Y/38 T.M.B.	ditto	
F	1 NCO 9 men	"	"	"	Officer & Y/14 T.M.B.	ditto	
G	1 NCO 9 men	"	"	1-0 PM 15-9-18	Officer & X/38 T.M.B.	ditto	
H	1 NCO 9 men	"	"	"	Officer & Y/38 T.M.B.	ditto	
I	1 NCO 9 men	"	"	"	Officer & Y/14 T.M.B.	ditto	

WAR DIARY
or
INTELLIGENCE SUMMARY.
(Erase heading not required.)

Army Form C. 2118.

Place: Sheet 57c
Appendix II d.

WORKING PARTY TABLE 15/16 - 9 - 18.

SERIAL Nº	STRENGTH OF PARTY	SUPPLIED BY	RENDEZVOUS	TIME	TO BE MET BY	NATURE OF WORK	REMARKS
A	2 Officers 70 ORs	114 Bde.	W10 B 5.8	8.30 pm 15/9/18	Officer of X/38 TMB	Carrying ammunition Bombs	As these parties report together. Battery representatives will meet them together carrying distribution of ammunition & minenwerfer.
B	do	do	W 3 a 5.2		" - Y/38 TMB	do	
C	do	do	W 4 A 1.5		" - Y/17 TMB	do	
D	1 N.C.O 9 ORs			8 AM 16/9/18	Officer of X/38 TMB	do	
E	do				" - Y/17 TMB	do	
F	do		W 3a 50 25		" - Y/38 TMB	do	
G	do			1 pm 16/9/18	" - X/38 TMB	do	
H	do				" - Y/17 TMB	do	
I	do				" - Y/38 TMB	do	

Appendix II d.
SAA 57/c

WORKING PARTY TABLE 17-9-18

SERIAL NO.	STRENGTH OF PARTY	SUPPLIED BY	RENDEZVOUS	TIME	TO BE MET BY	NATURE OF WORK	REMARKS
A	1 NCO 9 ORs	115 Bde	W.3a.50.25	8 AM 17/9/18	Officer of Y.17 TM Battery	Carriage of guns & ammunition	1. All those parties report together. Battery representatives will meet them together and arrange distribution amongst themselves.
B	do	do	do	do	Officer of Y.58 TM Battery	do	
C	do	do	do	1 PM 17/9/18	Officer of Y.17 TM Battery	do	
D	do	do	do	do			
E	do	do	do	do	Officer of Y.38 TM Battery	do	*2. Should a party not be required by O.C. Y.33 TM Battery it will be handed over to O.C. Y.7 TM Battery.
F	do	do	do	do			

16-9-18.

Wilson 2 Lt. RFA
for Capt. RFA.
DTMO 38th Div.

Army Form C. 2118.

WAR DIARY
or
INTELLIGENCE SUMMARY.
(Erase heading not required.)

Appendix III a.

Place	Date	Hour	Summary of Events and Information	Remarks and references to Appendices
			Sheet 57c.	
			LOCATION LIST.	
			EMPLACEMENTS.	
Battery			H.Q.	
X 38 T M Battery			W.4 B 10.70	W.10 B. 60 65 (3) ⎫ 18/9/18 W. 4 D 70.05 (1) ⎬ W. 4 D 95.90 (2) ⎭ Q 34 D 40.40 to Q 34 D 50.60 (6) ⎫ 19/9/18 Q 35 c 10.30 ⎬ 27/9/18 Q 35 c 20.35 Q 35 c 15.40 ⎭
Y 38 T M Battery			W.4 B 10.70	Q 35 D 22.85 Q 35 D 22.70 Q 35 D 18.99 Q 35 a 15.00

WAR DIARY or INTELLIGENCE SUMMARY.

Army Form C. 2118.

(Erase heading not required.)

Place **Sheet 57c**   Appendix III a

DETAIL OF TRANSPORT

No of Wagons.	Purpose	Rendezvous	Time	Remarks
4	Sundries	DTMOs HQ	4.0 pm 25th	
2	Ammunition	V.6.b.97	5.30 pm 25th	
4 (2 DAC 2 TMs)	Sundries	DTMOs HQ	4.0 pm 26th	
8	Ammunition	V.6.b.97	5.0 pm 26th	Two journeys will be made. Each battery will send back loading party of 1 NCO & 4 men to DUMP. by X.33 TM Battery will send Sergt. Green to take charge

WAR DIARY
or
INTELLIGENCE SUMMARY.

Army Form C. 2118.

(Erase heading not required.)

Place: Sheet 57c
Summary of Events and Information: Appendix III c

WORKING PARTY TABLE

Serial No.	Strength	Supplied by	Time	To report to	Rendezvous
A	1 N.C.O. + 15 men	2nd Divn.	8.0 A.M. 26th	X/38 T.M Battery	Battalion H.Q. Q.34.a.1.4.
B	do	do	1.0 P.M. 26th	Y/38 T.M Battery	
C	do	do	do	X/38 T.M Battery	
D	do	do	do	Y/38 T.M Battery	
E	2 Officers 50 men	do	8.0 P.M. 26th	X/38 T.M Battery	
F	do	do	9.0 P.M. 26th	Y/38 T.M Battery	
G	1 N.C.O. + 15 men	do	8.0 A.M. 27th	X/38 T.M Battery	
H	do	do	do	Y/38 T.M Battery	
I	do	do	1.0 P.M. 27th	X/38 T.M Battery	
J	do	do	do	Y/38 T.M Battery	

Army Form C. 2118.

WAR DIARY
or
INTELLIGENCE SUMMARY.
(Erase heading not required.)

Vol 28

WAR DIARY
OCTOBER 1918
36 Divisional Trench Mortar Batteries.

WAR DIARY or INTELLIGENCE SUMMARY

Army Form C. 2118.

Sheets 57C SE, 62C, 57B.

Place	Date	Hour	Summary of Events and Information	Remarks and references to Appendices
FINS	Oct 1		On the 1st October the unit was lying by FINS, nr 117.b. The next two days were also spent there, in rest and reorganisation. On the following day, at 3am a sector	
	2,3			
	4	3am	with Mobile Mortars went forward into action, but when they interfered owing to a broken axle in the gun carriage. Sufficiently of replacement this day	
EPEHY	5		the 1.E.O. of the unit moved to E.12.a. Mobile Mortar detachment with mobile mortars were again lying up by a broken axle. This party was attached to 113 Bty	
	7		On this date the H.Q. moved to Ravin. S.19.b (57B) That day the party with	
	8		mobile mortars fired upon irregular times in T.1.a.C.O. Sheet 57B, and they moved to base to AUBENCHEUL. On this date H.Q. of the unit moved to S.14.E.	
	9		On this date the Mobile Section reported to 19th St Bde at VILLERS OUTREAUX (Ref 57.B) and shipped it here to Malincourt, moving on again to BERRY	
	10		on the 10th, on which day 1820 of the unit again moved to CLARY - O.17.b.	
	12		The mobile party met with the base to TROISVILLES and reported to the 114 x 100 a.	
	13		St Bdes. That day of Lord guns forward as far as RAMBOURLEUX FARM	
	14		(K19.B.4.5.) that day the NaViry m. N14.d. was reconnoitred but no emplacement got put TM's. In this state HQ of the unit moved to TROISVILLES.	

WAR DIARY
or
INTELLIGENCE SUMMARY

Army Form C. 2118.

Place	Date	Hour	Summary of Events and Information	Remarks and references to Appendices
TROISVILLES	Oct.		Sheet 57 B.	
	14		The transport attached to the unit, lorries, was left at BERTRY for some days longer. Next day the mobile section put guns & lorries in the reserve in	
	15.		Rhyd. On the 17th O.15 O.R. were lent to 121 Bde. R.H.A. in exchange of lorry complete.	
	17			
	18, 19.		The next few days followed, and then on the 20th the mob. section took part	
	20th		in the Barrage for Infantry attack of 38 div. Three two Howitzers at the disposal of the B.M.O. Bde., and at headquins of mortars, targets were down on Monday 7 November T.	
	21.		The 21st was used at Troisvilles, and on the 22nd orders were received for the	
	22		mobile section to fire in conjunction with 23rd Jan. B. on an attack by 33rd & 21st Divs. on 38 TMB were to fire in closette, to be at the highest of 19 TM Bde thereby. On the 23rd The NC gave the schedule to the Sec. where though to complete the and finally what to do. A 33 Bde. who where in the front line played a considerable taking objectives. The section assembled at noon jours tournés.	
	23		midnight NG and fired at 2 am. expending 15 rounds in the barrage. Fired several rounds and were dueled with enough by the 33rd regiment by the North West at CAPREUX also by Bat. at TROISVILLES.	
	24th		We marched to CROIX & established dugout L.187.2. The mobile Section was billeted at CAUDRY.	

WAR DIARY or INTELLIGENCE SUMMARY

Army Form C. 2118.

Place	Date	Hour	Summary of Events and Information	Remarks and references to Appendices
CROIX	25th		Sheet 57 B. 1 Ret 51.	
			No change in dispositions, and nothing to report.	
	26th		Owing to casualties in the other units of 42 A, a statement was demanded by 114 B.G. regarding officers & other ranks available for other duties. Three officers & 20 OR's were shewn as available, and distribution was carried out accordingly. In this day in the 26th also, the Mobile Section shifted its Headquarters to S4h 37.30. & just in a named	
	27th		two Guns at C 30 a 30 50 & C 30 a 40.50.	
	28th		Nothing to report.	
	29th		The Mobile Section fired 440 rounds on targets S20 c 45 95 & 60 50 (Ret 51)	
	30th		Nothing to report.	
	31st		Orders were received, in view of operations pending, that all 2 mortars of the 58 TM B. should be got into action in the ENGLEFONTAINE sector — as many as possible by the 2nd Nov., with a view to systematic destruction of the hedges & enemy posts thereon up to the N.W. edge of the BOIS l'EVÊQUE NORMAL. Details will come under diary for Nov..	

6 Oct 1918
Capt RFA
Comp SFtin.

Army Form C. 2118.

WAR DIARY
or
INTELLIGENCE SUMMARY.
(Erase heading not required.)

Instructions regarding War Diaries and Intelligence Summaries are contained in F. S. Regs., Part II. and the Staff Manual respectively. Title pages will be prepared in manuscript.

Place	Date	Hour	Summary of Events and Information	Remarks and references to Appendices
Appendix 1				
	6" Newton TMs		Positions Barapi	
	do		K.14.d. 75.80	
	do		MG Nest at K.9.d. 95.50	
	do		K.14.d. 75.80	
	do		K.16.a. 60.65	
	do		K.28.a. 30.35	
	do		Sunken Road K.23.a. 00.10 – K.28.a. 20.35	
	do		K.28.a. 30.35	
	do		Sunken Road K.28.c. 70.70	

Army Form C. 2118.

WAR DIARY
or
INTELLIGENCE SUMMARY.
(*Erase heading not required.*)

WO 29

November 1915

War diary of 38th Divisional T.M. Batteries

WAR DIARY or INTELLIGENCE SUMMARY

Army Form C. 2118.

Place	Date	Hour	Summary of Events and Information	Remarks and references to Appendices
CROIX			Sheets 57B & 51.	
			On this date BTM's HQ were at CROIX (Sheet 57B, L.1.67.2) and Battery 1B on the line at F4b 37.30 (Sheet 57B). Preparations had already commenced in accordance with orders received on 31.10.18 for forthcoming Brigade operations against the FORÊT MORMAL. 12 guns in pits had been taken forward, and reconnaissances carried out of suitable areas for emplacements was formed on S25 & (Sheet 51) 240 rds of ammunition had also been carried forward. Infantry carrying parties worked for TMB's in the morning and a further considerable amount of ammunition was carried from CROIX in the afternoon.	
ENGLEFONTAINE 2.			During the day the 8 guns were in action. Smoke & H.E. guns employed are shown in Appendix G. (240 rounds were expended in a preliminary bombardment of Infantry objectives received by the enemy in S26 a.c. i.d. Brisk rifle fire followed from neighborhood of positions.	
	3.		200 rds were fired on hedges in S26 b & d. Infantry reported as very successful shoot. The enemy was caught unawares and great commotion caused in his forward area. Heavy retaliation followed upon enemy in front of our emplacements.	

Army Form C. 2118.

WAR DIARY
or
INTELLIGENCE SUMMARY.
(Erase heading not required.)

Instructions regarding War Diaries and Intelligence Summaries are contained in F.S. Regs., Part II. and the Staff Manual respectively. Title pages will be prepared in manuscript.

Place	Date	Hour	Summary of Events and Information	Remarks and references to Appendices
			Sheet 51 & 57A	
ENGLEFONTAINE	4.11.18		A bombardment which in support of infantry attack on the Fôret ST MARTIN took place. 200 rounds were expended. Heavy casualties were sustained by the unit, which are shewn in Appendix "I". Mobile Section from 38 MHB subsequently (Appendix II)	
		15.00	advanced in turn on road 18 & NW. Three mortars came into action at 15.05 hrs. Target being a house at B1 d 5.8 (Sheet 57A) which was manned by Germans. After 5 rounds fire ceased as our infantry were then attempting the action again succeeded in coming into action (at 15.15 hours) against Germans in high ground at B 7 b. 15 rounds were fired. The enemy fled.	
			The D/O of Minuit moved to ENGLEFONTAINE S 25 d 90.60. (Sheet 51) The Mobile Section reached LA TETE NOIRE T 23 d 90.60. (Sheet 51)	
	5.			
	6.		The A/Tst. H.Q. took out remaining guns, sorted and cleaned them. The mobile section moved to U 20 d 55.55.	
BERLAIMONT	7.8		H.Q. moved to BERLAIMONT. The mobile Section today reached ECUELIN D 5a (Sheet 57a) and moved on to HAUTTIGNIES (W 24 d 00.50.)	
	9.			
	10.		Men at HQ. were employed in cleaning rifles and equipment.	
	11.		Hostilities ceased at 11.00 hrs. The mobile Section withdrew to AULNOYE (Sheet 51)	

WAR DIARY
or
INTELLIGENCE SUMMARY.

(Erase heading not required.)

Army Form C. 2118.

Place	Date	Hour	Summary of Events and Information	Remarks and references to Appendices
NOYE	11		to which H2 also moved. Billets were occupied along the eastern side of road in U.2.F a & c.	
	12, 13, 14 Nov.		were spent in thorough rest at NOYE, in accordance with orders. The ensuing week was spent as follows. Marching and other drill was undertaken, and much attention was devoted to the thorough cleaning of equipment, transport and harness, as also to grooming and the improvement of condition of animals. Recreational training was taken up systematically and the unit took part in Rugby and Association football and in preparation for boxing competitions. The whole of these military and recreational activities however were interrupted by orders received to provide all salvage of ammunition in the	
ENGLEFONTAINE	21st		ENGLEFONTAINE AREA. In this the unit arrived on 21.11.15. C.O. & Adjutant & Recce Officer arrived from 38 Div H.Q. by the pastime	
	22nd		of the whole early morning reconnaissance of the area was commenced and transport from H.Q. the General Ammunition to a dump near SMECHES STATION (on X.46.c SheetS1A) March. The personnel was employed and	

WAR DIARY
or
INTELLIGENCE SUMMARY.
(Erase heading not required.)

Army Form C. 2118.

Place	Date	Hour	Summary of Events and Information	Remarks and references to Appendices
ENGLEFONTAINE	28 Nov.		Further men were obtained from our other Employment labour to assist in the work also obtained a regard to transport him on steady however. Employed at H.E.Q. Transport amount of ammunition was dispersed in all parts of the area (sectors) (FUTOY – ENGLEFONTAINE – PRIX DU NORD – VENDEGIES) and a very much larger body of men than of could have been fully employed. Splendid stores the were was carried on from day to day and although the challenge from some part of the men to the transport were practicable all vehicles did 2. 3 or even four journeys per day. The stand and the road were also very heavy to expected that absolutely failed to hold after torre or more	
	29 & 30.		The same work was proceeding with the assistance of the late drawn attached to U/S H.M.B.	

O. Somers
Capt. RFA
A.P.O. 38 Div

WAR DIARY
or
INTELLIGENCE SUMMARY.
(Erase heading not required.)

Army Form C. 2118.

Place	Date	Hour	Summary of Events and Information	Remarks and references to Appendices
Appendix I			2 huns at S.25.d.65.65	Appendix II 676309 Gnr R J Munro Injured	2-11-18
			1 " S.25.d.65.70	5113 Gnr D Downie Wounded Remained at duty	2-11-18
			2 " S.25.d.95.95	16644 Bdr W Hughes Wounded in action	2-11-18
			2 " S.25.d.75.50	113081 Gnr J Wilson "	2-11-18
			S.25.d.95-50	4123 Bdr N H Watts "	4-11-18
			S.26.a.00.00	43648 LBdr J Petts "	4-11-18
			S.26.a.10.00	315556 Gnr J A Simmons "	4-11-18
			S.26.a.15.05	249383 Gnr W Irwin "	4-11-18
				49 Gnr H J Patton "	4-11-18
				140571 Gnr J J Jonno "	4-11-18
				Capt 460 Bhy R.F.A. "	7-11-18

O J Town
Capt 27/11

WAR DIARY
or
INTELLIGENCE SUMMARY.

(Erase heading not required.)

Army Form C. 2118.

WAR DIARY
of
38TH DIV. T.M. BATTERIES
DECEMBER 1918

Army Form C. 2118.

WAR DIARY
or
INTELLIGENCE SUMMARY.
(Erase heading not required.)

Place	Date	Hour	Summary of Events and Information	Remarks and references to Appendices
ENGLEFONTAINE			Sheet 51.	
	1/6		The whole month will the 28th went to sent in the	
	28		duties of occupation on the outpost line with	
	28		On this date the unit marched to LE QUESNOY	
LE QUESNOY			Entrained entrained for AMIENS area	
CORBIE	30/5		Unit arrived & billeted at Corbie	

D J Jones
Capt RFA
DTMO 38th Division

Army Form C. 2118.

WAR DIARY
or
INTELLIGENCE SUMMARY.
(Erase heading not required.)

War Diary

38th Dn. T.M Batteries

January. 1919.

Army Form C. 2118.

WAR DIARY
or
INTELLIGENCE SUMMARY
(Erase heading not required.)

Instructions regarding War Diaries and Intelligence Summaries are contained in F. S. Regs., Part II. and the Staff Manual respectively. Title pages will be prepared in manuscript.

Place	Date	Hour	Summary of Events and Information	Remarks and references to Appendices
CORBIE	1-2/19		Demobilisation commenced	
BEHENCOURT	23/1/19		Orders received to reduce to cadre strength — 31-1-19	
			War Diary closed.	
	31-1-19			
			O.S. Foster	
			Capt R.F.A.	
			D.T.M.O. 3rd Division	

(A9475) Wt W.335/P560 600,000 12/17 D. D. & L. Sch. 52a- Forms/C2118/15.